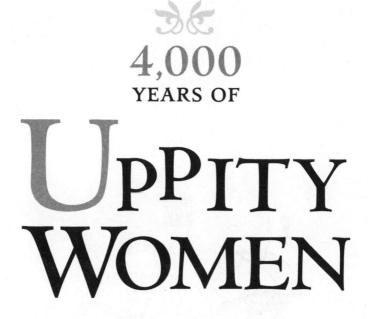

4,000
YEARS OF

UPPITY
WOMEN

Rebellious Belles, Daring Dames,
and Headstrong Heroines
Through the Ages

VICKI LEÓN

MJF BOOKS ❧ NEW YORK

Published by MJF Books
Fine Communications
322 Eighth Avenue
New York, NY 10001

4,000 Years of Uppity Women
LC Control Number: 2011932141
ISBN-13: 978-1-60671-086-9
ISBN-10: 1-60671-086-9

Page 3: *Iraq: Lyre with Bull's Head*,
The Granger Collection, NY. All rights reserved.

Page 128: *A Game of Chess* (Sofonisba Anguissola, 1532–1625),
Erich Lessing/Art Resource, NY.

All other art © 2011 JupiterImages Corporation.

Printed in the United States of America.

MJF Books and the MJF colophon are trademarks
of Fine Creative Media, Inc.

QF   10   9   8   7   6   5   4

To Paul Anders Ogren,
who delights in the printed word,
the perfect Brugmansia, and
the planet's uppitiest women
—a loving thank you.

C O N T E N T S

PART FOUR

UPPITY WOMEN OF THE NEW WORLD

LATE 1500S–1899

ᴇᴠᴀ 159 ᴀᴠᴜ

Bibliography

ᴇᴠᴀ 211 ᴀᴠᴜ

Index

ᴇᴠᴀ 215 ᴀᴠᴜ

INTRODUCTION

Over the last 4,000 years of recorded history, uppity women have rocked as many cradles as the other gals, but they've rocked a lot of boats as well. Although the women in this book come from different cultures, eras, and social classes, they all share a common bond: They didn't buy into what others said that women could and couldn't do. These high-energy risk takers with attitude knew how to leverage the pluses they were born with—which often weren't many.

During the last 40 years, while researching and writing about these women, I've come to see that truly uppity women have other traits in common. These include the flexibility to roll with whatever life offers up; unquenchable vitality; lion-heartedness; everyday courage—the kind I call gumption—and a rollicking sense of humor, even when events in life hit below the belt, as they often do.

In every single generation of the 4,000 years this book spans, there have been innumerable women who did remarkable things. Even way back in the B.C. centuries, irrepressible females broke all kinds of barriers. They ruled. They invented. They cured people. They killed people. They ran cities and businesses. They won races, athletic and political. They explored. They bankrolled explorers. They even bankrolled religions! Almost every organized religion, from Christianity to Buddhism to Quakerism, has gotten off the ground thanks to the hard work and cold cash of women. Within these pages you'll meet Fabiola, an early Christian who established the first free public hospital in the Western world—and hit the street to collect dying patients herself. You'll get to know Katie von Bora, the gal who housebroke Martin Luther—and kept him afloat by running multiple enterprises—and many others.

Some chose notoriety over niceness and autonomy over social and sexual conformity. You'll encounter women who relished the good fight, and others who blithely wallowed in the bad ones, from pirate gal pals Mary Read and Anne Bonney to South America's nun turned top gun, Catalina de Erauso.

The Calendar and the Clock

Keep in mind that the periods we call "medieval" and "Renaissance" would be meaningless to the women (oh, yeah, and the men) living in them. They are labels we've invented for our convenience, and the four eras covered in our pages—ancient, medieval, Renaissance, and New World—overlap each other. Another thing: People in centuries past didn't slice up their hours and days like we do, or keep track of them as meticulously. That makes most of the dates in this book mushy. The B.C.–A.D. divide is another artificial device. Until fairly recent times, folks kept track of large swaths of time via reccurring events, such as the Olympic Games, or they named periods of time after elected officials or rulers. In grimmer circumstances, time was marked by plagues and disasters, such as the Starving Time endured by the unlucky British colonizers of Jamestown, several uppity women among them.

In the index, you'll find each woman listed by her name, her geographic home base, and the date she was active, defined here as age 30, more or less. The entries also give indicators of time.

These Gals Got Around

This book represents a world stage: It bursts with women from around the Mediterranean Sea but also from around the globe, from Iceland to South America, Asia to Africa, Boston to Budapest. You may be surprised to learn that numerous gals on the go were jet-setters long before there were jets. They started young, too—take the famous track star sisters of the first century A.D. and the daredevil teens on horseback who out-Revered Paul Revere during the American Revolution.

Photo I.D., Please

One headache of historical research is pinning down names, an especially fraught problem when it comes to women's names. There is little agreement about the proper spellings of the names of the women in this book. Until a century ago, even in the United States, people were casual about the spelling of their names and of others' names as well. This relaxed attitude extends and expands back in time, compounding the problem. That situation, plus the fact that women have often shed surnames as they marry and remarry, quickly makes women invisible in history. Additionally, many cultures had the habit (some still do) of naming their girls Julia 1, 2, 3, or of drawing from a very small pool of acceptable names, which makes it even harder to trace someone back through time. (Check out the endless Macedonian Cleopatras and Roman Julias to see the real complexity.) Finally, for centuries history books and printed matter often sidestepped female names, referring to individuals as "wife of," "said to be the mother of," and my personal favorite, "a woman who. . . . " Some still do, alas.

Women Lost and Found

Given that women become invisible over time, you may wonder how I unearthed this brawny batch of 200-plus trailblazers (drawn from a stockpile of more than 1,500 women of long ago that I've profiled). I've had to become a historical detective, chasing clues however faint and unconventional. Many of my entries are drawn from extant primary sources, ranging from writings of the period to coins, artifacts, graffiti, music, portraits, legal transcripts, love notes, and hate mail. You'll see this source material mentioned in many of the entries—plus more details in the bibliography, including online information and further resources.

Even today, there is a general belief that women of long ago did little of real importance. Worse is the belief that if they did do something of value, they left little behind as evidence. Not true! As I will continue to repeat on these pages and rant to audiences everywhere, the proof about our foremothers, even those in the deep past, exists—it just takes persistence and legwork to wangle out all the material, often contradictory, and sort it into a pattern. Instant-access materials, such as Wikipedia and Google search results, are invaluable, as long as you know they represent the beginning of a search, not the stopping point.

What You Will and Won't Find Here

These entries illuminate the lives of flesh-and-blood girls and women. Amazons, goddesses, legendary Helens of Troy, and literary figures may get a mention in passing, but real females are what I choose to write about. I don't take a sweetness-and-light approach, either. You'll get a tart appraisal of these formidable females, chosen for the fullness of their stories, the offbeat nature of their triumphs (and/or downfalls!), and the sheer audacity and variety of their accomplishments. You'll find a few headliners here: Joan of Arc, Cleopatra, Elizabeth I. Since they already get so much attention, I burrow around, looking for women of humbler station. Before our modern era, there wasn't much of what we'd call a middle class; nevertheless, a surprising number of uppity entrepreneurs created one as they went about inventing themselves. Within these pages, you'll meet some of them: French publishers, Pompeiian loan sharks, New Orleans voodoo queens, and Egyptian alchemists. Highfalutin poets and female philosophers mix it up with early porn artists and professional poisoners. You can sample Hittite psychologists and Sumerian beer-brewers, big-hearted philanthropists, and early American doctors and ferryboat operators who got paid in tobacco.

Here's to Women

For decades, I've struggled to define the ultimate uppity woman of long ago, but historian Pauline Pantel beautifully beat me to it. She once wrote, "Slowly, very slowly, women became individuals, people whose consent mattered." What an uplifting, penetrating phrase: *People whose consent mattered.* That distills what women of long ago fought for and what we, their descendants, continue to claim today. This book, an omnibus of female iconoclasts, written in their irreverent spirit, is dedicated to every one of those unquenchable trailblazers, and to you, dear reader. I welcome your comments at www.vickileon.com.

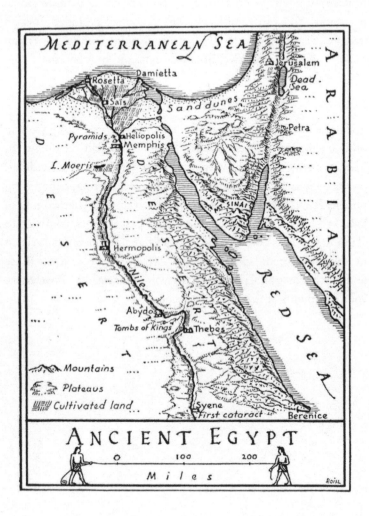

MEDITERRANEAN SEA

ARABIA

Jerusalem

Dead Sea

Damietta

Rosetta

Sand dunes

Sais

Petra

Pyramids

Heliopolis

Memphis

L. Moeris

SINAI

DELTA

Hermopolis

Nile

RED SEA

DESERT

Abydos

Tombs of Kings

Thebes

EGYPT

~~~~ Mountains

Plateaus

Cultivated land

Syene

First cataract

Berenice

ANCIENT EGYPT

0   100   200

Miles

Roisl

PART ONE

UPPITY WOMEN

OF

ca. 2500 B.C.–A.D. 450

❧❧❧❧❧❧

CASPIAN SEA

TAURUS MT.

Tarsus

Carchemish

Arpad
Aleppo

Nisibin

Van

IRAN PLATEAU

Nineveh

Assur

MEDITERRANEAN SEA

Palmyra

Euphrates

Tigris

Sidon
Tyre
Damascus

DESERT

Upi

Tumail

Ctesiphon
Kish

Babylon

Jerusalem

Gaza

Nippur

Dead Sea

Petra

Susa

Eridu

Ur

Elat

Present shore

MT. SINAI

PERSIAN GULF

RED SEA

Cultivated land

ANCIENT MESOPOTAMIA

Scale 0 ___ 300 Miles

Roiss

Tunes in Old Mesopotamia

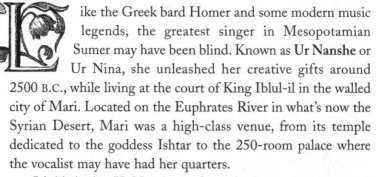

ike the Greek bard Homer and some modern music legends, the greatest singer in Mesopotamian Sumer may have been blind. Known as **Ur Nanshe** or Ur Nina, she unleashed her creative gifts around 2500 B.C., while living at the court of King Iblul-il in the walled city of Mari. Located on the Euphrates River in what's now the Syrian Desert, Mari was a high-class venue, from its temple dedicated to the goddess Ishtar to the 250-room palace where the vocalist may have had her quarters.

It's likely that Ur Nanshe performed religious hymns as well as songs that lavishly praised her ruler. Besides singing, she played the lyre and harp; for encores, she danced. Limousines may not have lined the block back then, but musicians did get fussed over. Their ailments got special attention at a clinic for warblers; they also enjoyed a daily wine ration, which might further explain the need for a clinic.

Although Sumerians had no Grammys to give out, they honored their musical celebs. While excavating Mari, French archaeologist André Parrot discovered several statues of this superstar, with her signature long black hair and brilliant blue eyes. Her images, now in Syria's Damascus Museum, bear the simple inscription, "Ur Nanshe, the Great Singer." Now, that's enduring fame.

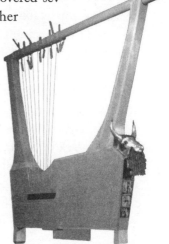

Instead of YouTube, Sumerian singers and musicians were showcased on musical instruments like this lyre.

Brewing Up a Dynasty

T he Sumerians, who lived between the waters of the Tigris and the Euphrates rivers in flat, jalapeño-hot Mesopotamia (mainly present-day Iraq), loved two things: list-making and beer. Man, woman, and child, the Sumerians loved their barley suds. They even had a slogan: "Beer makes the liver happy and fills the heart with joy."

In ancient times, the water was of a dubious quality likely to make your whole system unhappy. Thick barley beer, on the other hand, was relatively germ-free and nourishing, too. Since it was unfiltered, the Sumerians had to drink it through a tube.

Women dominated the entire beer cycle. They brewed most of it. They sold most of it. And they drank their fair share. **Kubaba**, an unassuming but clearly sharp lady (also referred to as Kug-Bau or Ku-Bau), kept a tavern and/or brewery in the independent Sumerian city-state of Kish, about 55 miles south of modern Baghdad. Then, as now, taverns had a rep for rowdiness, rigged prices, and watered drinks. Although priestesses no doubt got as thirsty as the next Sumerian, they were forbidden by law to stop by for a cool one. Penalties were a bit stiff: death! Nevertheless, as ration lists found by archaeologists show, the priestesses drank beer daily. (Perhaps the barkeeps made beer runs to the temples.)

Kubaba had higher ambitions than pulling drafts and running a pub. No one is sure how she managed to become queen of Kish, but she gained the throne about 2500 B.C. (That far back, the lack of detail isn't unusual—no one really knows how Sargon the Great went from his humble origins in Kish to a stint as one of Sumer's most famous kings, either.)

No splash-in-the-beer-barrel, one-term ruler, Kubaba rose to highest prominence and stayed there. Her sons succeeded her, and the dynasty she founded lasted for 100 years. During her tenure, according to the few records that refer to her, Kubaba "made firm the foundations of Kish." That sounds like earthquake retrofitting, but it may mean she extended political control over another part of Sumer. In Kubaba's day, Kish had dominance over both rivers, and thus controlled irrigation to crops and cities downstream. Kish is traditionally known as the first city to politically control all of Sumer.

But Kubaba never forgot her tap-house background. On the surviving official Sumerian kings' list found in an ancient text called the Esagila Chronicle, she called herself simply "Kubaba the beer woman." In contrast to the bombast of most ancient rulers—"Yo! Pay attention! I'm the greatest!"—that shows class.

Some years ago, a University of Pennsylvania educator and a beer manufacturer collaborated to make barley bread (using barley malt, honey, and dates), ferment it, and produce an ancient Sumerian beer they named Ninkasi, after the goddess of the brewery. An audience of adventurous beer-lovers at a micro-brewery convention in 1989 drank the brew in the Sumerian fashion, just as Kubaba would have done, through large straws or tubes. It was pronounced "sweet, fruity, and full-flavored."

Beer-making women knew how to keep cool while they mashed sprouted barley, bread, and sweetener into thick brew.

Career Scribe

Becoming a scribe in old Mesopotamia was the B.C. equivalent of law school: costly, slow, and male dominated. Women, such as **Amat-Mamu**, could elbow in but they had to be from a scribal family or the upper class. Besides writing and reading, student scribes learned arithmetic, geometry, and higher math from sunrise to sunset. A key task was to measure things: Scribes did surveying, divided up estates, and mediated between parties on property and legal matters.

And they took inventory. Folks in Sumer and other parts of Mesopotamia invented writing primarily so they could keep track of their stuff—and other people's stuff. They also dreamed up a written script called cuneiform, with 600 symbols just to make things challenging. Instead of paper, they used the cheapest, handiest material available—wet clay. Clay tablets may sound clumsy to us, but talk about durable: Many of their writings have survived more than 4,000 years.

Amat-Mamu was a career scribe whose 40-year tenure spanned the reign of King Hammurabi in the 1700s B.C. She lived and worked in a cloister of priestesses in Sippar, an important city and religious center about 40 miles from Babylon. This was no backwoods operation: The cloister held more than 140 priestesses, plus supervisors, slaves, janitors, scribes, and cooks. It sounds like a tough joint to break out of, but convent life was pretty laid back. The priestesses,

Sumerians loved to jot things down, from to-do notes to inventory lists. They used a stylus to make cuneiform symbols on clay.

many from noble families, could come and go freely. A few were even married. None, however, was allowed to have kids; for that function, Sumerians had modern-sounding surrogate moms (usually the sister of a priestess or a concubine).

Priestesses at Sippar didn't have much down time. They transacted much of the city's business, handling property management, buying and selling slaves, and taking care of legal matters. Who do you suppose provided the documentary backbone for all of this feverish activity? Amat-Mamu and her scribal crew, of course. To the Sumerian mind, if it wasn't on clay, it did not exist. Almost everything we think of as administration passed through her busy hands— temple records, for example, showing what was sacrificed or gifted to the sun-god Shamash, when, and by whom. (Religious centers accumulated goods and property at an astonishing clip.)

In her long career, Amat-Mamu came to oversee the work of other scribes, most of them women. She didn't know it at the time, but she was leaving us a treasure. Most of what we know about Mesopotamian women and men comes from the life work of Amat-Mamu and her fellow scribes. This treasure trove includes everything from laundry lists and legal briefs to school papers, personal letters, love songs, and curses.

Rough on Slackers

ow we know where that tongue-in-cheek term of endearment "old battle-ax" came from: **Queen Aahotep**. An Egyptian royal who wed her brother as tradition demanded, Aahotep gave birth to sons Ahmose and Kamose, later ruling with them. Aahotep didn't really mind motherhood—but military action, planning battles, and crushing rebels were her meat and drink.

Around 1580 B.C., the Hyksos invaded Egypt. These northern tough guys used horse-drawn chariots in battle. Not about to be left behind by new technology, Aahotep and the royal family hastily ramped up, soon fielding their own war-chariot divisions from Thebes, their capital. Aahotep took up her wartime role with relish. There was one aspect of military life, however, that the queen could not abide: army slackers. She took special pride in going after them herself, administering a fearsome justice. Archaeologists have discovered stone inscriptions at Karnak that brag about Aahotep's role: "She has looked after Egypt's soldiers; she has brought back her fugitives and collected together her deserters; she has pacified Upper Egypt and expelled her rebels."

For her deserter-decimating efforts, Aahotep was three times given the Order of the Golden Fly, an award for bravery. (To Egyptians, the fly represented tenacity—a trait the queen clearly nailed.) In Aahotep's intact tomb at Thebes, researchers found her trio of 24-carat trophies on a necklace, along with—what else?—a gorgeously decorated ceremonial battle-ax, now on display in the Cairo Museum.

A battle-ax herself, Aahotep used her weapon on deserters.

Fake Beard, Genuine Pharaoh

gyptian dynasty dating is still very slippery, but somewhere between, let's say, 1512 and 1479 B.C., Thutmose III, the nephew of **Hatshepsut**, may have muttered a few unkind remarks about how his aunt kept him on hold for decades as a pharaoh-in-waiting.

As the first woman to become a full-on pharaoh, Hatshepsut took advantage of two things: her innate shrewdness and her dynastic luck. When her dad, the first Thutmose, died around 1518 B.C., she married her half-brother Thutmose II and became queen of Egypt. It seemed a normal strategy to bolster his right to govern—or so Thutmose II thought. It's possible that Hatshepsut had other goals. For 14 years of co-rule, she led, he followed. The only thing they collaborated on equally was daughter Neferure.

When Thutmose II died, Hatshepsut sprang into action as regent for the young heir, Thutmose III, her husband's only son, produced by a harem girl. After a couple of years, with zero bloodshed or fuss, she left mere queenship behind and became female king of Egypt, taking on the five titles of a pharaoh, the male clothes, the weird gear—even the false "beard of wisdom" each pharaoh wore. To clinch her silky smooth transition, Hatshepsut gained the support of key officials, including Senenmut, the highest-ranking man, who tripled as steward, architect, and longtime tutor to her daughter Neferure.

Pharaoh relaxing on the weekend: no beard required.

On paper it was still a dual reign, and to make the family connection tighter, Hatshepsut had Neferure marry young Thutmose III. As compensation, mother gave daughter the best hand-me-down she could think of: the title Divine Wife of Amun, which carried various real-estate perks. Thutmose, meanwhile, learned to toughen up and lead men by becoming a military commander.

With the help of Senenmut, the female pharaoh built a three-terraced temple, a propaganda piece she called "a garden for my father [the god] Amun." Set against the sheer coral-colored cliffs at Deir el-Bahri, the temple later became famous for medical cures. Hatshepsut also put up two spectacular 100-foot-tall obelisks of red granite in Karnak to glorify Amun.

A farsighted businesswoman, Hatshepsut mapped a daring itinerary for a trade expedition through a waterway on the site of today's Suez Canal and south along the coast of Africa to the land of Punt. When her fleet successfully returned with a tangy cargo of cinnamon, myrrh trees, ebony, ivory, panther skins, ostrich eggs, and live baboons, the canny pharaoh sent more expeditions to the Sinai Desert for turquoise and to the African continent to collect wild animals for her new garden of Amun zoo.

When Thutmose III finally followed—or pushed out—Hatshepsut after 22 years of rule, he may have tried to hack every mention of her as female king from the face of Egypt. But he couldn't or wouldn't obliterate Hatshepsut's name and image entirely, and statues and inscriptions of her name still exist in quantity.

The most recent conclusions from historians about the fascinating story of Hatshepsut lean toward a middle path, interpreting her ascension to pharaoh as less a power grab than as a family obligation, perhaps to protect the throne from unfriendly forces while Thutmose III was still young. Historians have also acknowledged Hatshepsut's artistic legacy, noting that her prosperous reign set new standards of craftsmanship and originality in sculpture, bas-relief murals, and, most of all, architecture.

Astute Player from Punt

Pudgy, pint-sized **Queen Ety**, nicknamed the Princess of Punt, stood tall on the 15th-century B.C. world trade scene. For Ety and Perehu, her lean Jack Sprat of a husband, life was good: They had a lock on the frankincense and myrrh trade.

Their homeland of Punt probably sat on the eastern Horn of Africa and the western tip of Arabia, straddling the Red Sea. Its poor soil, rocky ravines, and gasping hot climate weren't good for much, but they suited the thorny myrrh bushes and the scraggy frankincense trees just fine. Frankincense (meaning "true incense") and myrrh were the diamonds of the ancient world. Day and night, temples from Babylon to Greece burned quantities of both resins to please the many deities around the Med. The fragrant white smoke was also used to fumigate homes, clothes, latrines, and sickrooms. Myrrh had key medicinal uses as painkiller, wound dressing, and burn remedy. Demand for both was high, and supply was limited to a fortunate few lands, whose rulers created a monopoly on the stuff for thousands of years.

Fashion statement of Punt's pint-sized queen: a see-through skirt and not much else.

To harvest the incense, Queen Ety's workers tapped the sap from the trees, collecting the gum that formed days later; other workers sorted the beads and grains of gum for sale. Myrrh and frankincense plants grew wild in just two remote places, and the belief that nei-

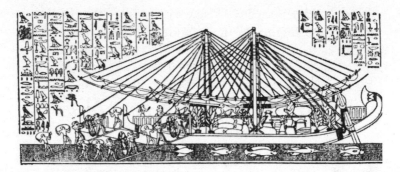

Ety and company sold incense by the boatload.

ther plant could be domesticated made both gum resins even more valuable.

One fine day around 1469 B.C., Queen Ety saw five 60-foot ships near her shores, with Egyptian harps hanging from their masts as a peace signal. The fleet belonged to Hatshepsut, the much-talked-about female pharaoh of Egypt. Although the Egyptians lived a long and difficult sail away from Punt, they ran through incense like you wouldn't believe. Ety and company no doubt rubbed their hands in glee, anticipating a huge reorder.

What Queen Ety soon learned was that her Egyptian dream client was planning to do some botanical cartel-breaking. Egypt was spending too much on imports and Hatshepsut had decided to grow her own. Besides the quantities of frankincense and myrrh loaded into the ships' holds, the order also included live plants: thirty myrrh trees, carefully roped to contain their root balls.

Did Queen Ety maintain her virtual monopoly, or did Hatshepsut succeed in her plans to grow locally? Accounts differ. According to one, the temperamental shrubs failed

Ety's Egyptian customer Hatshepsut wanted to grow her own myrrh trees.

to thrive outside Punt. Another report said that some plants growing in Egypt's capital of Thebes flourished; although the plants vanished long ago, the holes carefully prepared for them have been found by archaeologists. The trees planted at the pharaoh's own complex across the Nile River definitely took hold; the gnarled roots can still be seen in front of Hatshepsut's temple.

Another astonishing thing that came out of the trip to Punt was artistic immortality for Queen Ety and her entourage. An Egyptian artist accompanied the expedition. He made drawings of the fleet, the myrrh trees, the Puntites, and the inimitable Queen Ety herself—all of which ended up as striking reliefs painted on the temple walls at Thebes and at Hatshepsut's temple of Deir el-Bahri, where some can still be admired today.

The Beautiful One Has Gone

 t's not a stretch to call Egypt's **Queen Nefertiti** the Jackie Kennedy of her day. An international household name, she didn't just set fashion—she *was* fashion. Her imagery showed up everywhere in Egypt: on wall reliefs, statues, busts, rings, and scarabs. Cameras would have loved her telegenic profile and the jazzy blue turban she made hers alone.

A commoner like her aunt, Queen Tiye, who was wife of Amenhotep III, Nefertiti emulated her aunt by also marrying a man who became pharaoh, Tiye's son. But a huge philosophical and spiritual gap existed between Amenhotep III and his son— and between Tiye and her glamorous niece Nefertiti.

Nefertiti, whose name means "the beautiful one has arrived," and the lantern-jawed, baggy-bellied man she married were big-picture thinkers. Their goal? To break from the mummified weight of the past and create an Egyptian Camelot, where arts, culture, and religious worship could take on new vitality and freedom. It was a big menu, but this bold, brainy, and unusually demonstrative pair of leaders relished the challenge.

Encouraged by Nefertiti, who took an active role in the top-to-bottom changes, Amenhotep IV tossed aside the old lineup of gods and focused on Aten, the sun god. Nefertiti and her husband, now calling himself Akhenaten ("living spirit of Aten"), were the only ones allowed to serve the god; this meant pink slips all around for the huge priestly population. The royal family and court left the capital of Thebes for a brand-new garden city dedicated to the sun god. Now the el-Amarna archaeological site, the short-lived new city was called Akhetaten, or Horizon of the Sun God.

Why is it that Camelots always seem to have more than their share of tragedy? Three of Nefertiti's six daughters died young, political pressures made life increasingly difficult for her, and perhaps Akhenaten began to backpedal in his new beliefs. That is but one theory of what came between this couple; the clues are incomplete and contradictory, so it's a guessing game anyone can play. What we do know is that in the 12th year of her husband's reign, Nefertiti's name simply vanishes from the record, replaced by that of one of her daughters as Great Royal Wife. Nefertiti was a woman who got more attention and public exposure than Jackie O. What happened? The beautiful one has long gone, but the mysteries surrounding her remain unsolved.

Egypt's fashion plate, the Jackie O. of her time.

"All in the Family," with a Twist

onsanguineous marriage, a term that means "keep the royal blood in the family at all costs," led to some pretty weird carnal arrangements in ancient Egypt. **Ankhesenamun,** who couldn't have seen more than 22 birthdays in her life, may take the cake for the strangest string of sex partners.

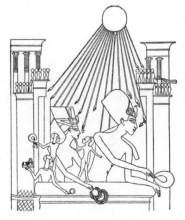

Ankhesenamun was a happy youngster, playing with her sisters in the warm light of the sun god.

The third daughter of Queen Nefertiti and Pharaoh Akhenaten, she grew up in a rollicking family group. As children, she and her sisters ran about naked, their hair in a traditional topknot. In the garden city of Akhetaten, life was sunny in their new palace. Like her sisters, however, Ankhesenamun had to mature pronto. When her older sister Meritaten died, it was Ankhesenamun's turn to do her dynastic duty. In rapid-fire succession, she had to marry (and bury) her pharaoh father, her uncle Smenkhare, and finally Tutankhamen, who was all of nine years old. The too-knowing teen no doubt felt more like his sister—which she also was.

Their marriage lasted ten years, until Tut's death in his late teens, and apparently produced two babies, neither of whom survived. By now, Ankhesenamun was pretty fed up with the notion of consanguinity. She also feared there was worse in store. For years a shady figure behind the throne had run things more and more. It was her grandfather, Ay, a powerful commoner and the father of Nefertiti.

As the priests began Tut's mummification and funeral arrangements, the young widow knew she had just 70 days (Tut's embalming period) to find a new husband. She hatched a desperate plan. She sent an urgent message to Suppliliumas, the Hittite king to the north of Egypt, that said: "My husband has died, and not one son do I have. I've heard you have many—will you send one to be my husband? I will never accept marrying one of my servants."

When he received it, the Hittite king, amazed yet suspicious, made inquiries about the reliability of her offer. Meanwhile, the clock was ticking on Tut's embalming.

Exasperated and fearful, Ankhesenamun shot off another message, saying, in essence, "This isn't a mass mailing! I haven't asked anyone else—just you. Send me a spare son pronto, and I'll make him my husband and king of Egypt!"

Convinced at last, the Hittite king sent his son Zannaza to Egypt. Tragically, the young prince was intercepted and killed before his arrival. The clock ran out; Ankhesenamun was married to a 60-year-old whom she considered despicable and beneath her, grandfather or not. At Tut's funeral Ankhesenamun, already wed to Ay, placed a wreath of flowers on her dead young husband's forehead. It was the last documented act of a courageous girl who had lived too much, too soon.

But an Egyptian princess had to grow up fast— often to marry her brother or her own father.

With a Little Help from Her Friends

Back in the 12th century B.C., or thereabouts, **Deborah** doubled as an early Golda Meir and Moshe Dayan for the Israelites, providing political and military leadership against the dastardly Canaanites. In Deborah's time, the Jews were a loose group of recently nomadic clans trying to muscle their way onto some land so they could quit being homeless. They were about as patriarchal as you could get: Females were good for begetting, and that was about it. So how the heck did Deborah get to be a judge and war leader and end up with her very own song in the Bible?

She began as a prophetess or seer. Second sight was looked on with favor by the Jews and other ancient folks; people with the gift seemed tighter with the Almighty, making their advice more valuable. Seers often functioned as tribal leaders, which seems to have been the case with Deborah. She and her husband lived on a well-traveled road between the towns of Ramah and Bethel, and locals constantly came to her for advice.

Big worries loomed for Deborah and her people, however. The enemies who had been pounding on the Jews for 20 years threatened to eliminate them entirely. The worst menace? The cutting-edge army of Sisera the Canaanite, whose 900 iron chariots and many archers were making chopped liver out of the Israelites in their camps.

Deborah's powerful skills made her a natural choice to become an Israelite judge, a word more akin to "deliverer" or "war leader" in those days. To start, Deborah got troop commitments of 10,000 men from various tribes and assigned a seasoned fighter named Barak to head the army. A keen

To do today: Whip Canaan, write hit song.

strategist, she saw that the Canaanites already held the plain below Mount Tabor and she devised a squeeze play.

Barak seemed to lose heart. "I'm not going to go unless you do as well, Deborah."

She replied along the lines of, "No sweat. I'll lure them to the river, and you sweep down from the north and push them to me."

The armies' arrival at the river neatly coincided with a monster rainstorm, which made the already marshy ground a mess. Result: 900 chariots stuck in the mud, Canaanite soldiers put to the sword, Israelites victorious.

There was just one loose end: That scoundrel Canaanite general Sisera managed to slink away from the chariot debacle. Luckily for the Israelites, Sisera slunk into the vicinity of a goat-herding gal named **Jael**. A quick thinker with excellent upper body strength, she lured him into her tent, then gave him a good smiting with her mallet and tent-stake.

Soon thereafter, Deborah paid tribute to soul sister Jael in the 31 verses of the "Song of Deborah and Barak," an evergreen hit of the Old Testament, sung around Jewish waterholes and campfires for millennia.

Dynamic Hittite CEO

oyal families of ancient times often arranged weddings the way we order pizza—for convenience.
Occasionally, however, the marriage came with,
shall we say, extra toppings. **Queen Puduhepa,**
whose life partner gave her respect, love, and a
lavish amount of legal latitude and shared power, entered one
such marriage with "the works."

This happened in Hittite country around 1258 B.C., when
the Hittite kings controlled a huge chunk of what is now Turkey.
To the south, their pharaoh counterparts ran Egypt. These two
superpowers of their day often jockeyed over the terrain between
them, Syria and the Holy Land.

Daughter of a priest, Puduhepa grew to womanhood in the
town of Kizzuwatna. She'd been a high priestess of Ishtar for
years when she married King Hattisili and went to live in
Hattusas, the capital of the Hittite empire. They reigned
together for 24 years. "Together" is no exaggeration. There was
no wretched first-lady circuit of tea parties, hospital openings,
and rubber-chicken dinners for Puduhepa. As queen, she had
legal rights to intervene in affairs of state, stand in for her husband when he was away, and administer royal properties.

Well educated, interested in literature and Hittite history,
ambitious for her family and country, Puduhepa carried on a
busy international correspondence with her royal counterparts
(male and female) in Egypt and elsewhere. Archaeologists have
found 15 letters to her from Pharaoh Ramses II. She also signed
the king's letters with her own royal winged sun-disk seal; four
of her personal seals have turned up in excavations.

Every country longs for peace and prosperity in its time, and
the Hittite nation was no exception. After years of negotiation
and dowry-dickering, the formerly warring Hittites and

Egyptians signed a peace agreement called the Treaty of Kadesh. Versions of it still exist in Egypt and Turkey; a silver version of the treaty was signed with Puduhepa's personal seal as well. The treaty culminated in the marriage of Puduhepa's daughter Naptera to Ramses II. The queen further busied herself with achieving dynastic marriages for her other children.

The archaeological riches of the Hittite capital have yet to be completely excavated. The letters, legal documents, inscriptions, and other writings that have already come to light reveal that the Hittites had developed immensely sophisticated systems, such as wage and price controls, a body of written laws, rules for social conduct, and religious rituals for every activity. At Hattusas there are rock reliefs that show Puduhepa performing religious rites to the Hittite thunder god. The letters and inscriptions portray a likable, human side to the royal couple. Puduhepa's husband, Hattisili, for instance, says this about his marriage: "God granted us the love of husband and wife, and we had sons and daughters."

How Hittites Achieved Mental Health

bout 1300 B.C., in Hittite lands that would one day be called Turkey, career opportunities for early psychologists (only mature women need apply) were booming. With their deep beliefs in the power of ritual, the Hittites relied on a vast number of practitioners to carry out the intricate religious and magical rites that governed every aspect of their lives. The generic job title for these positions of importance was surprising: Old Woman.

Masdigga was one such Old Woman practitioner in

Kizzuwatna, a Hittite-controlled coastal town about 200 miles south of Hattusas, the capital city. Masdigga used a repertoire of psychological techniques to solve problems ranging from family quarrels to impotence. For anger management or marital conflicts, she might prepare a tongue-shaped package of mutton fat and wool and burn it over a fire, while telling the troubled patients how to let go of anger. Some of her rites were much more elaborate: For tension and worry about enemies, she conducted a weekend seminar ritual to enlist helpful angels, banish personal woes, or chase her clients' problems into the frontal lobes of people they didn't like.

Patients with anger issues? Hittites knew how to handle 'em.

The props Masdigga needed for one round of sympathetic magic required a veritable scavenger hunt: wine, quantities of cord, a bowstring, loaves of bread (baked and unbaked), pine cones, six kinds of metals, a tree, three colors of wool, live mice, and various other live and butchered animals.

Besides solving personal difficulties, Masdigga and her professional peers were routinely called in on national issues. When a plague hit, for instance, Hittites tended to believe that one of their gods had fallen down on the job or was neglecting them. The remedy? Get the god's attention with a really nice spread of goodies, and then send that plague on its way by transmitting it to the correct victims—for example, those non-Hittites down the road. At times, the Old Women corps also directed their ceremonial ire toward the gods of Hittite enemies, clearly at fault for a given pestilence or natural disaster. Masdigga also made contracts and other documents legally binding by using the supernatural powers vested in her to swear to their authenticity.

Since currency was little used in those times, an Old Woman invoice got paid in goods, the excess mice and other props being recycled back into her practice. Luckily for us, the Hittites loved to document their actions. Details about Masdigga's career and the storehouse of knowledge she drew upon were meticulously documented on clay tablets that provide a written treasury about a fascinating people. Over 70 texts of their rites have been recovered from archaeological endeavors.

A History Buff Like Her Dad

nnigaldi began life simply as the beloved daughter of Nabonidus, the last home-grown king of Babylon and Ur before the Persians took over. Most Babylonian kings went in for blood sports like war and lion-hunting, activities that translated well onto heroic murals. Nabonidus had a contemplative side. An antiquities-restorer and history buff, he loved messing about with ancient artifacts and taught Ennigaldi to appreciate them as well.

Twenty-five hundred years after Ennigaldi and her dad lived, archaeologists excavated parts of their palace and temple complex at Ur. As they worked, they were puzzled to find dozens of artifacts, the ages of which varied by hundreds of years, neatly arranged side by side. Later, clay drums with signs in three languages showed up—the first known museum labels. It's now thought that Ennigaldi and her father may have personally excavated some of the pieces in the museum she maintained—artifacts that were already antiquities in her day!

This museum miss found it possible to handle more than her curator's job because she didn't have a commute. The palace complex included living quarters, the museum structure, a temple, and a school for priestesses, run by—and possibly taught by—Ennigaldi. By her day around 550 B.C., this school had been in continuous operation in the same spot for 845 years. Its equipment and teaching techniques resembled those of other schools—although with young priestesses as students, there may have been less emphasis on the corporal punishment that formed part of the normal school curriculum in that time and place. In 547 B.C., Ennigaldi got a third job; moonlighting, literally, with the moon. She became a high priestess of the moon god Sin (also called Nanna) and spent nights of religious significance in a small blue room on top of the great ziggurat of Ur.

In Mesopotamia, male and female literacy was pretty much reserved for the upper classes. Literate women, however, had their own written dialect called Emesal. Because of its differences, archaeologists and linguists can tell when women wrote—or were written to—on the cuneiform tablets.

Babylonian correspondence: a letter inside an "envelope" of clay.

When Babylonians talked about correspondence, they didn't say, "Did you get my letter?" Instead, they would ask, "Did you hear my tablet?" We have yet to hear any tablets from Ennigaldi; but tomorrow, perhaps, an archaeologist's spade may unearth some Emesal words direct from this dynamo of ancient Ur.

Persian Payback

y 550 B.C., King Cyrus the Great of Persia had carved out an empire from the Mediterranean Sea to India. After whipping the Assyrians, he looked around for an even tougher opponent. Everyone agreed that would be the Massagetae, nomads of Scythian stock who lived between the Araxes River and the Caspian Sea. Their ruler, **Queen Tomyris,** served as commander-in-chief of the fearsome Massagetan army, and her grown son, Spargapises, was second in command.

At first, Cyrus figured he'd conquer the widowed Tomyris with a simple-minded ploy. Setting up his army camp at the river, he sent her a marriage proposal. Meanwhile, his troops were busy building bridges across the water. Knowing the Persian king was hot to possess her lands, not her body, Tomyris responded with acid politeness: "Cyrus, my advice is to forget about the Massagetae—just rule your own people and try to handle the sight of me ruling mine." She added, "On the other hand, if you want to fight, fine. Either we'll invade you, or you invade our territory, on this side of the river."

Cyrus's circle of advisors unanimously urged him to let Tomyris and her army cross the river. But then his old buddy Croesus piped up. The filthy-rich king from Asia Minor, who'd already gotten thumped by the Persians, Croesus played the deadly male wimp card to Cyrus. "It'd be a disgrace to give ground to a mere woman!" Croesus proposed a trap: Set up camp on Tomyris's territory. Bait it with a few feeble troops, plus a huge banquet of beef barbecue and potent Persian wine for the Massagetan boys, who were known to eat anything and were unused to alcohol. (They preferred to get high at their wingdings by inhaling the smoke from burning marijuana seeds.)

Tomyris fell for the ruse. She assigned a third of her troops to her son, who fell on the camp, slaughtered the small contingent of Persians, and attacked the bait, soon becoming sated and drunk. After that, it was a piece of cake for Cyrus's troops to kill the Massagetae and take the son prisoner. When word reached

Proud Persian King Cyrus the Great thirsted to conquer Tomyris. He drank a bloodbath instead.

Tomyris, she fired off another note: "Cheap shot, Cyrus. Return my son and get out of my country—or I swear I'll give you more blood than even you can drink."

Meanwhile, back in the Persian camp, Tomyris's son had asked to have his bonds removed. Before they knew it, the kid had committed suicide. Now his mom had even more reason to be steamed.

With Tomyris at its head, the Massagetae took on Cyrus's much larger army, first with bows and arrows, then hand-to-hand, with bronze spears, daggers, and battle axes. By the end of one of the most violent battles the world had yet seen, tens of thousands of Persians, including Cyrus, lay dead. At the conclusion of that long and bloody day, Tomyris's troops looked for the king's body. When they came to her with the corpse, Tomyris filled a wineskin with human blood. Pushing his face into it, she said, contemptuously, "Still thirsty for Scythian blood, Cyrus? Go on—drink your fill!"

Much to Be
Philosophical About

P hilosophy as a career choice today is about as imprac-
tical as you can get. In ancient times, however,
philosophy was both a comfort and a natural outlet for
women. The mentor system prevailed; women studied in a
variety of ways, with every sort of philosopher. Here's a peek
at four very different lives.

Some 2,300 years before the Beatles, a heretofore proper
young thing named **Hipparchia** did it in the road. The occasion
was her wedding to Crates, Athens' most popular street philosopher. Instead of drooling over wedding gifts, Hipparchia got
into the Cynic lifestyle, writing diatribes, raising two kids on
beans three times a day, and engaging in outrageous behavior.
(To show their disdain for convention, Cynics performed bodily
functions in public that are best left to the imagination.)
Forming a partnership of equals, Hipparchia and her mate also
counseled the sick and troubled, arbitrated quarrels, and consoled the bereaved. Their diet wasn't 100 percent beans, either.
This marital tag team worked the dinner party and symposium
circuit, where Hipparchia debated with and enraged the mostly
male crowd—another poke in the eye of convention.

If Greece had given MVP (Most Valuable Philosopher)
awards, **Arete** would have walked away with one. This cerebral
philosopher from the Greek city-state of Cyrene in North
Africa had awesome stats: 35 years of teaching, 40 books to her
credit, and the ultimate in-group compliment—many of her
pupils became philosophers themselves. Arete learned her chops
from her dad, Aristippus, who studied with Socrates but
believed in pleasure as the greatest good. Her daughter espoused
an egalitarian philosophy unusual for the times, dreaming of a

world with neither masters nor slaves. Arete's prize pupil was her own son, nicknamed "Mother-taught," who followed her as head of her school.

In sixth-century Crotona, a rich Greek colony on Italy's coast, **Theano** and her daughters lived a Pythagorean life, a modern-sounding holistic philosophy that combined healing, music, exercise, a vegetarian diet, child psychology, and mental health studies with physics, geometry, astronomy, and other disciplines. Theano ran the school and commune developed by her husband, Pythagoras, after his death. A writer, thinker, and healer, Theano epitomized the sexual morality and serene appreciation for other living things for which the Pythagoreans were famous.

By 300 B.C., the Greek philosopher Epicurus had groups of disciples from Athens to Lampsacus in Asia Minor (Turkey today), where **Themista** and her husband, Leontius, lived. She was a distinguished student—and maybe more. In a note that would make any philosopher's heart beat faster, Epicurus wrote to her: "I'm quite ready, if you don't come to see me, to spin thrice on my own axis and be propelled to any place you agree upon." Perhaps they had a metaphysical ménage à trois. At any rate, Themista named her son Epicurus, and the philosopher returned the favor by dedicating his book *Neocles* to her. As an author, Themista was also held in high esteem by Greeks and even by the early Christian fathers, who normally sneered at pagan philosophy.

Female philosophers made many kinds of music.

First Woman to Win Olympic "Gold"

Daughter of a Spartan king and sister to another, **Cynisca** was born into a life of privilege that bored her. Being a mere land baroness did not appeal, either, although 40 percent of the land in the huge city-state of Sparta was owned by women like her. In Sparta's militaristic society, girls had a longtime tradition of wrestling, running, riding horses, and bathing nude in icy rivers with the boys. It sounds healthy and independent to modern ears—but the Spartans mainly sought fit mothers and healthier babies to make future soldiers.

Early in life, Cynisca became horse-happy, breeding and training her own animals. She is said to have begun lobbying her brother Agesilaus to let her enter a four-horse chariot in the upcoming Olympic Games, or perhaps it was the other way around, since sources emphatically do not agree. It seems likely that she wanted to hold the reins herself, as Spartan women commonly did in daily life. Whether she got to remains ambiguous. Xenophon, an ancient source, says Cynisca's kingly brother persuaded his sister to try for the Olympics. His motive, Xenophon claims, was to show that chariot racing was proof only of wealth, not "manly virtue." Whatever *her* motives, Cynisca took first-place wins at least twice, in the Olympics of 396 and 392 B.C.

Besides a hero-shrine in Sparta, that honor entitled her to place a life-size bronze statue of herself and her horses at the temples of Zeus in Olympia and Sparta. Its inscription exults: "Sparta's kings were fathers and brothers of mine; victorious with my chariot of swift-footed horses I, Cynisca, have erected this statue. I declare myself the only woman in all Hellas to have won this crown. Apelles son of Callicles made it." Cynisca deserved a good gloat. Thanks to her and the five or more women emboldened to follow her lead, Greek women went from *being* the prizes at athletic contests in Trojan times, to taking them. The inscriptions and the black stone base of Cynisca's statuary still exist, on display in the Olympia Museum in central Greece.

Serpents: Sexier Than Husbands?

If **Queen Olympias**, the brilliant, hagridden mother of Alexander the Great, had lived in our times, her obsessions with husband, son, slinky toys, and female rivals would have delighted psychiatrists. As an 18-year-old, this fiery princess from Epirus met King Philip II of Macedon at a Bacchic mystery-religion affair, where initiates got happy with the gods through ecstatic dancing and snake-handling. Olympias and Philip married in 357 B.C. At first, her fixation with serpents didn't seem weird per se. After all, throughout Greece and Macedonia, snakes (outdoors or in) were greeted with enthusiasm. They were not only good rat-catchers, they were thought to bring good luck as well.

As first lady and main maenad (female follower of Bacchus) of Macedon, the teen queen passed along her snake-charming enthusiasm to the local women. Okay, her husband could handle that. But when Philip discovered that Olympias kept her own bunk cozy with a reptile or two while he was off fighting, it was a major anti-aphrodisiac. Although he was notorious for having other bed partners, at least they were *mammals*.

As even an amateur shrink could see, the high-strung Olympias lacked outlets for her brains and ambition. As time went on, she became merely one of Philip's wives and spent most of her days terrorizing the other spouses. Her reputation for rages kept the world at arm's length, including her son, Alexander, who kept in touch mainly via correspondence. When he died at age 32 in faraway Babylon, his mother was in Macedonia. As Olympias found, snakes may have lovely qualities, but they are low on solace.

Alexander the Great

The queen's hobbies: son Alex and strange bedfellows.

Surf and Turf Piracy

The wild land of Illyria didn't have much to brag about in the third century B.C. First of all, no one could pinpoint exactly where it was (some people have the same trouble with its current counterpart, Albania). It did have one saving grace: its pirate industry. Greek and Roman victims alike agreed that Illyria's pirates were far worse than anyone else's. Thus, it was understandable that **Queen Teuta**, the newly widowed leader of the

Illyrians, really took offense when the Romans started whining about establishing some maritime laws, including making piracy a felony.

"Piracy a crime?" she huffed. "We call it our private citizens' right to seize booty at sea without interference from their government." Teuta further proclaimed, "What a bunch of wet togas you are. You want me to destroy what some Illyrian tribes call a legitimate way of life."

As head of this unruly tribal society, she was just trying to keep unemployment rolls down. In her day, pirates often were recruited from the ranks of out-of-work mercenaries. People have to make a living somehow, was her philosophy.

Teuta was a planner with expansive ideas. Her recently departed husband, Agron, had fielded a fleet of 100 swift ships. She went him one better, giving "plunder away!" letters to existing pirates, and assembling a larger fleet and a huge land army and sending them off with instructions to regard everything as fair game. They took Epirus; they pillaged Issa; they plundered Epidamnia. Teuta kept this up for several years, sending out another batch in 229 B.C. to terrorize the island of Corfu.

The Illyrians were dandy fighters, organized in well-armed mobile units. Finally, however, Rome got ticked off enough to raise large land and marine forces and quell them. In 228 B.C., Queen Teuta finally caved. She sent envoys to Rome to conclude a treaty that included a fixed yearly tribute payment. That and other restrictions ended Illyria's fun on the bounding main. Teuta's story may sound fanciful, but archaeologists have located a gravesite inscribed with her name in modern-day Albania.

No Chick-lit, but Genres Galore

Prolific **Pamphila** of Epidaurus, who lived during Nero's era, the first century A.D., might feel at home in our world of trivia book top-ten lists. The wife and daughter of scholars, Pamphila chose a less lofty path, writing 33 encyclopedic collections of odd facts, riddles, and anecdotes. We still have tatters of her trivial pursuits, scattered throughout the random ramblings of Athenaeus, Diogenes Laertius, and other ancient writers.

In Tanagra around 500 B.C., **Korinna** competed lyrically with fellow Greek Pindar, a poet idolized by Olympic Games winners who paid him big coin to write gooey paeans of praise about their feats. Nevertheless, in poetry-slam competitions, Korinna's local legend-spinning and use of clean, simple verse beat Pindar's work five times in a row. In his graceful loser's speech, Pindar is said to have called her "a sow." After hearing her rival's pretentious purple poetry, Korinna snarkily suggested, "Try sowing [metaphors] with your hand, not the whole sack [of grain]." Fragments of her work are extant in the Loeb Greek lyric poetry collections.

Calling you a sow, Korinna, doesn't make me a sore loser!

Sulpicia, a Roman poet who produced sensual poems around 25 B.C., worked from red-hot experience. She had her first love affair as a 20-something single living under her uncle's roof, and chronicled it from shout-it-from-the-rooftops rapture to the wrenching discovery that her man had another woman. A bouquet of six of her bold and beautiful poems survives, found hidden within the writings of the poet Tibullus.

Earthy Greeks, so quick to extol the delights of male-to-male eroticism, so blasé about bestiality, incest, and other deviant deeds among their gods and goddesses, were pretty tight-lipped about the idea of females writing porn. So it comes as no surprise that males had a fit when **Philaenis** of Samos, possibly a courtesan of the third century B.C., pro-duced the first X-rated sex guide for the

Men need new pickup lines. The first chapter of my book is "How to Make Passes."

complete voluptuary. Revealing everything from indecent kisses to sex positions to the best aphrodisiacs, her book showed how, why, and where. The book begins by explaining "How to Make Passes," and moves into "Seduction by Flattery." Tragically, only small shards of Philaenis's work have been recovered by archaeologists amid the scraps of the Oxyrynchus papyri—but they can actually be seen online in Oxford's papyrology exhibition.

Saucy Bizwomen B.C.

arly Alexandrians were brilliant at inventing oddball devices. A local barber, fooling around with pulleys, pipes, and compressed air, dreamed up a musical gizmo called a hydraulis or water organ. Quite taken with its sweet, reedy notes, his wife, Thais, learned to play its keyboard. Soon the joyous sound of the water organ was heard around the Mediterranean. By Imperial times, hydraulis musicians wowed the crowds at weddings, theater intermissions, and other events. The instrument's popularity encouraged Nero—emperor and wannabe artiste—to take it up. Thais's tuneful achievement may have started a trend toward women hydraulis players, even in the most appalling of settings. Incongruously, it became the favored instrument to accompany gladiatorial matches. Sometimes backed by a horn or two, the organist (usually female) ground out old favorites while gore-covered combatants ground against each other.

Asellina, a Pompeii business woman, ran a brothel and greasy spoon. Outside her joint, a sign bearing a dice cup and four phalluses let passersby know that the first floor had booze and gambling, the second story the shady ladies. Asellina's establishment was a sign of the cosmopolitan nature of the Roman world in the first century A.D. The upstairs-downstairs gals came from all over Greece and North Africa. The tavern walls (now excavated) were covered with their names and lusty quotes from the regulars, who included a customer called Scordopordonicus, or Garlic Fart. Although Asellina's employees were mostly slaves, they took an active role in politics by decorating her building with candidates' slogans, urging the thirsty male electorate to vote. Nearly everyone, Asellina included, got into local politicking. Only the candidates themselves stayed mum—not a blessed sound bite in the bunch!

Pompeii may not have had charge cards, but it had rapacious moneylenders. Among them was **Faustilla**, who gained a certain dark prominence for her hard-nosed business dealings. Lenders worked out of gaming dens and taverns, often using the walls in lieu of paper documents. Faustilla hung out at several dives in rotation, and archaeologists have found her transactions on various walls around town. In a typical day's work she made loans of 15 and 20 denarii, charging monthly interest that ran a painful 45 percent per year. No slouch in the collateral department, either, this entrepreneur collected earrings, a clock, and a hood from one desperate female client as security against her loan. These details were duly noted on walls that survived the destruction of Pompeii in A.D. 79—proving that loan sharks really *do* live forever.

Seeking Stone, Discovering Milestones

Alchemists were a wild-eyed, often paranoid bunch on a mystical quest to discover the philosopher's stone, a key ingredient of the pseudo-scientific recipe for changing mundane matter into something rare and valuable—preferably gold. The forerunners to modern chemists, alchemists did indeed stumble on a variety of invaluable inventions, processes, and chemical properties as they chased a chimera.

The clear standout among them was a woman known variously as **Mary Prophetissa**, Maria of Alexandria, and Mary the Jewess. In her search for alchemical solutions, she succeeded in perfecting a variety of instruments and substances with real applications to chemistry. Among them were the prototype of the still, whose usefulness for making alcohol and perfume soon became apparent; and the kerotakis, a device that used the principle of reflux cooling to treat metallic objects with vapors. Her name is linked to the discovery of hydrochloric acid, and to the black alloy niello. She's frequently cited as the author of a now-lost work called the *Dialogue of Maria and Aros on the Magistery of Hermes.*

The alchemists' secret symbol for summer.

The symbol for winter.

Maria had the good fortune to live and work in Alexandria, Egypt, which for centuries was a city of exploration and experimentation. Its patrons the Ptolemies lavished money on science and art. Its artisans developed the fields of metallurgy and glassblowing to exacting standards, while the engineering minds of the city and visiting geniuses like Archimedes made it a hotbed of exciting discoveries.

Among her accomplishments, Maria invented a utensil that has been a must-have in kitchens for 2,000 years, the double boiler. Cooks throughout Europe still have a folk memory of Mary the alchemist, remembering her in the varied names given to her invention: *bagno Maria* in Italian, *baño María* in Spanish, and *bain-Marie* in French. Although alchemy would prove to be a dead end, adepts like Maria enabled true chemistry to emerge.

Vinegar ("*vinum mortuum*")
Gold.
"*Calcinatio Auri*" (*burning gold to ashes.*)
Silver,
Copper ("*Venus*").
Antimony,
Mercury,
Iron ("*Mars*").
Sulphur ("*Father*").
The elements (air, earth, fire, water)

496

The Cleos, Mom and Daughter

Unjustly labeled as a glamorous party animal and a grand schemer, **Queen Cleopatra VII** (*the* Cleopatra) was also a bookworm, a linguist, and a pretty darn good mother. She had four children—a boy with Julius Caesar, and two sons and her namesake daughter with Marc Antony.

After the spectacular life and suicide of her megastar mom, the daughter, **Cleopatra Selene** (Cleo Moon), was all but forgotten to history. After being orphaned, she and her twin brother, Alexander Helios (Alex Sun), were rescued by Octavia, the kind-hearted sister of Octavian (Augustus), and grew up in Rome.

At 15, Cleo Selene met and fell in love with an older royal orphan from North Africa: Juba II of Mauretania. Octavian, now Emperor Augustus, was all smiles, pleased and relieved to offload Cleopatra's daughter. Giving Cleo Selene a large dowry, he appointed her Queen of Mauretania. After she wed Juba, they went to live in the kingdom he'd been ripped away from as a child. Juba and Cleo Selene ruled Numidia and Mauretania, where they raised two children and reigned tranquilly for many years. Coins issued in her name show that Cleopatra Selene honored her Greek and Egyptian roots. She and Juba are buried in a huge, handsome domed mausoleum that still stands in Algeria, near Algiers.

Cleopatra knew how to roll out her negotiation skills.

Track Trio on the Pro Circuit

he first century A.D. was a time of glory for the athletes **Hedea**, **Tryphosa**, and **Dionysia**, three talented sisters from Tralles, a prosperous, sports-mad city overlooking the Maeander River in Asia Minor (Turkey today). By this time, almost every city in the far-flung Roman Empire boasted public baths, gymnasia, and running tracks. Each year, more than 300 athletic competitions (and musical ones, as well) were held around the Mediterranean and Black Seas. The number of athletic meets and female participation in them grew yearly. Good Roman roads had made overland travel safe (if slow), and a reduction in once-rampant piracy made marine travel another option.

Tryphosa and Dionysia, the oldest and youngest of the triple-threat trio, specialized in running. Hedea was an all-rounder. Besides track, she raced war chariots, sang, and played the lyre.

The sisters competed in two types of events: crown and money. Crown games included the original big four: Olympian, Pythian, Isthmian, and Nemean games. Instead of medals, winners got high-status symbolic wreaths. Once the winning athletes were back home, the perks flowed, such as free meals for life. At money games, winners got cash and other gifts, paid for by the sponsoring city. First prize in the 200-meter footrace, for example, could amount to four times the annual salary of a soldier. Goodies aside, athletes also won incredible fame.

The teenagers' record of wins is astonishing. Over a period of some five years, Typhosa took crowns at the Isthmian Games near Corinth and the next Pythian Games at Delphi—the first girl ever to do so. Dionysia won track firsts at the Asclepeian

Festival in Epidaurus and the Nemean Games. Hedea won the war-chariot race at the Isthmian Games and two firsts for track at the Nemean and Sicyonian games. She also nabbed a first for lyre players at the Sebasteia Festival in Athens. These "golds" are only career highlights; the formidable sisters no doubt racked up many seconds and thirds, but in ancient times, only first-place winners got recorded or rewarded. The girls were made honorary citizens of several cities, including Corinth. Citizenship (which women lacked in certain times and places) gave such benefits as the right to vote, tax-free pensions, and office-holding privileges.

Hedea, Tryphosa, and Dionysia may not have endorsed track shoes, but they surely served as role models for girls everywhere. They were probably active through their teenage years. By the time they retired from competition, the words from a certain Paul from Tarsus, an evangelist and rabid sports fan, were on everyone's lips: "I have fought the good fight; I have finished the course; I have kept the faith." His quotes could just as easily have summed up the lives of the track trio from Tralles.

Most of what we know about these girls comes from the existing base of their now-lost statues, erected at the famed oracular shrine at Delphi

Long-ago teens competed athletically and musically.

by their father, Hermesianax of Tralles. Further confirmation comes from the historian Pausanias, who saw and wrote about their still-intact monument 100 years later. This proof sheds substantial light on women's competitive athletics in the Mediterranean world of the first century A.D.—and adds to the growing evidence about female participation in athletic, musical, and cultural life 2,000 years ago.

Relative Remover

If business cards had been in vogue in ancient Rome, one of them might have read, "**Locusta** is the name, poison is my game." It's surprising how many people needed the services of a professional poisoner: patricians who'd run through their money and wanted to hurry along that inheritance from dear old uncle; men going for marriage number three who found it tough to repay the dowry of wife number two; and the platinum card customers—emperors, empresses, next-in-lines, and other wannabes.

Rome had a tradition of female poisoners. At a trial in 331 B.C., 20 noblewomen found guilty of killing their husbands insisted they'd been brewing a tonic. Asked to prove it by drinking the stuff in court, they did and died on the spot.

Locusta, however, was no one-shot amateur. From the Roman province of Gaul (modern France), she'd gravitated to Rome, where the action was. For years, she was reputed to be on retainer for one royal or another. Being a pro had its ups and downs: a few prison terms, a couple of death sentences, and an equal number of lucky, 11th-hour reprieves.

Locusta's first big career break came from Empress Agrippina the Younger, who'd married her uncle Claudius and put up with him until her cherub Nero was 17, when she gave Locusta a call. The women fixed on mushrooms, one of Claudius's favorite foods, as the vehicle. Despite Locusta's most toxic efforts, however, the dose of 'shrooms gave the emperor the runs instead of eternity. Since pros always have a backup plan, the emperor promptly received a fatal dose of poison on a feather down his throat.

The next year, Locusta's career as celebrity poisoner got another boost. Nero, who had succeeded his stepfather as emperor, had a teenage royal rival, his stepbrother Brittanicus. Nero deemed it only fitting that this sole surviving son of

Claudius should join his father in the meat locker. In a bravura move involving sleight of hand with a water glass, Locusta had young Brit taken out at dinner, right in front of his family, friends, and the official food taster. Nero was so thrilled with the results that he gave Locusta choice real estate and referred clients to her. He also awarded her a full pardon for her prior poisonings, a few of which were still on the books. Ever the entrepreneur, she launched a select school for poisoners, whose graduates went on to pharmaceutical successes. (Locusta was rumored to have caused more than 10,000 deaths but that may have been advertising puffery.)

In A.D. 68, a fed-up Roman Senate issued an order to have Nero killed the old-fashioned way—that is, stripped naked and beaten to death with iron rods. Even though Nero always kept a box of Locusta's finest at his bedside for such eventualities, he was forced to flee and kill himself in a most inartistic manner— with a dagger.

But all bad things, not just Nero, must come to an end; that year proved lethal for Locusta, too. In the brief reign of the next emperor, she and other high-profile villains were smartly marched through the city to an execution so efficient that even a pro poisoner could not find fault.

Corpse creation while you wait.

Early Kilroy: Julia and Sabina Were Here

For six years, **Empress Sabina** took part in one of the world's great love affairs. Her only gripe was her role: voyeur. As Roman empress, she got to watch the very public amore between her 50ish but frisky husband Hadrian and a pouty-lipped young stud named Antinoös. How did perky, sweet Sabina get into this jam? Match-making by her Auntie Plotina, the prior empress, had hooked her up with an unenthused Hadrian. Theirs was a superglue marriage, however, stuck together for three decades, during which Sabina's supply of cheerfulness congealed into bad temper.

Despite mutual detestation, Sabina and the restless emperor often traveled together. In A.D. 130, Hadrian, Antinoös, Sabina, and her adoring friend **Julia Balbilla** took a Nile River cruise through Egypt. One night, Antinoös went for a dip in the Nile that proved to be his last. Hadrian went nuts with grief. Before the cremation ashes were cold, Hadrian declared his boy-toy from the Black Sea a god—a first for a young nobody. A chain of temples to Antinoös soon opened around the Mediterranean.

Sabina's pal Julia had a tiny gift for poetry and a big talent for sycophancy. As she said, what should have been a glorious tour became a nightmare because that loopy kid had to get himself drowned—incredibly thoughtless. Julia and Sabina longed to see the big draw onshore: the "singing" Colossi of Memnon, two 60-foot statues of an ancient pharaoh that each morning drew a crowd hoping to hear the mythological Memnon speak to his mother, the dawn goddess. Finally, the women went sans emperor, still moping over his boyfriend. The statue "sang" on cue (actually making a loud cracking noise), and the two ladies added their autographs to the statue's leg. Most visitors were content to deface by scrawling name and date. Not Julia! Seeing the chance for poetic immortality by self-publishing on a literal hard copy, she wrote a five-verse poem praising Memnon, Sabina, the emperor, and herself. She wrote the darn thing in the antique Greek of Sappho, dead more than 700 years. Believe it or not, her obnoxious twaddle can still be seen on the battle-scarred calf of Memnon's statue, 1,882 years later.

Undaunted Until the End

esides a well-oiled brain, **Beruria** of Tiberias had moral fiber. In ancient times, she was one of the few Jewish women allowed to study the Talmud, the body of commentaries on the Torah, sacred writings of the Old Testament. A true scholar and teacher, she could, it was said, "read 300 laws from 300 masters in a day."

Her legal views and wise homilies, which were also quoted in the Talmud, are still known today. In one story, when villainous men antagonized her husband, Rabbi Meir, and he prayed for their deaths, Beruria called him on it. "God wants the destruction of sin, not the sinners," she counseled. "Pray for their repentance."

The couple's young sons both died suddenly one Sabbath. So as not to grieve the rabbi on a holy day, Beruria waited until the day of observance was over, and said to him: "Some time ago, a man left some jewels of value in my trust; now he's called for them. Shall I return them?"

Meir responded, "Of course," and she showed him the two small corpses. As he cried, she reminded him, "Didn't you say that we must return to the owner the precious jewels he lent us?"

Beruria had to be tough to survive. She lived in second-century-A.D. Palestine during the harsh reign of Roman emperor Hadrian, who forbade religious rites, closed schools, and exiled or killed Jewish sages. Among his martyrs were Beruria's mother and her father, Rabbi Hanina ben Teradion. Beruria had to witness her dad's death on a pyre of green brush, hideously drawn out by the dousing of the flames with water.

Despite these tragedies and others, Beruria continued teaching. Sadly, her reputation as a principled intellect was marred by malicious commentary circulated about her death. According to this account, one of her husband's students nearly succeeded in seducing her. It is said that the incident revealed Beruria's own weakness to herself, and she committed suicide. The most disturbing part of the anecdote? Her husband, Rabbi Meir, supposedly put the student up to it in order to test his wife and prove to her that prejudice against women had a basis in fact.

*The challenge of Talmudic
study didn't defeat Beruria; her
husband's betrayal did.*

No-fault Deflowering

udging by statistics on women who join religious orders, career chastity seems to be losing ground in today's world. Two thousand years ago, though, the job of vestal virgin was a very coveted position in Rome. Since the misty beginnings of the Eternal City, six vestals had the chore of tending the Sacred Fire of Vesta, goddess of the hearth. Young girls, six to ten years old, from good families competed for the slots. If those kids let the fire go out, an unspecified but very bad disaster would befall Rome.

Julia Aquilia Severa may have been the most famous vestal of all time. In July of A.D. 218, she and the other vestals had the fire blazing, but a major disaster hit town anyway. His given name was Varius Avitus, but he became informally known as Elagabalus. Fourteen years old, freakishly dressed in bangles, eye paint, and a long gown described by an eyewitness as "a nightmare of purple-and-gold silk," he flounced into the city with a sacred black stone in tow, drawn by six white horses. He was Rome's new emperor.

One of several unforgettable scions in a wacky dynasty of mother-and-son rulers from Roman Syria, Elagabalus adored religion and left politics to his mom, Julia Soaemias, and grandmother, Julia Maesa. As high priest of Elagabal, the Syrian sun god, the kid wanted to introduce the Romans to their new deity without delay. So the teen emperor shucked his current wife, had the sacred fire transferred to a gleaming new sun god temple, and picked Aquilia Severa for his bride in 219. This was a bit like choosing Mother Teresa to play the lead in the pop star Madonna's life story. As he explained, "I'm marrying Aquilia so that godlike children might spring from me, the high priest, and her as high priestess."

As luck would have it, young E. got terribly busy, attending debaucheries, marrying and divorcing two other women, and having affairs with charioteers, and could not follow through on his dynastic plans. By March of 222, the emperor and his mother had raised the disgust level to such an extent that they were beheaded by the Praetorian guard, dragged through the streets in another sort of parade, and thrown into the Tiber River.

After what she'd been through, Aquilia probably longed to return to vestal virgining. Vestals, however, had strict rules of chastity; if one deliberately broke her vow, she was buried alive in a special chamber with a lamp and a brown-bag last supper of bread, milk, oil, and water. To check their vows, the high priest periodically ran a "neck test" on the little vestals. As even the dimmest Roman knew, the thyroid gland of a virgin expands after the first act of intercourse.

Through no fault of her own, Aquilia was now missing the vital equipment of a vestal virgin. Perhaps they gave her early retirement instead of requiring her to finish the standard 30-year vestal career. She'd certainly been through enough to try a saint.

Rome's Wild-card Enemy

 n the third century A.D., **Zenobia Septimia**, an Arab queen, devised a simple but elegant plan to split the Roman Empire (at that time a vast sprawl from Spain to Armenia) in two. This formidable ruler made her home in Palmyra, a fashionable city of 150,000, full of colonnades, fountains, palaces, and marble temples, glittering like a mirage in the cinnamon-colored Syrian desert.

The key to the economic success of the City of Palms can be summed up with two words: silk and taxes. Like a well-positioned spider, Palmyra sat where key trade routes intersected, happily reselling silk and other rare goods and collecting taxes—a privilege earned by its site as a buffer state between the Roman and Persian empires.

Zenobia claimed descent from one of the early Cleopatras, which would give her a meld of Macedonian Greek and Arab blood. Although historians of old habitually labeled famous women "beautiful, chaste, and clever," it may have been an understatement in Zenobia's case. She also loved to ride and hunt. Married at 14, she had just six years with her husband, King Odaenathus, before he was mysteriously killed.

Zenobia was not the first vigorous Arab queen in ancient times. She followed in the footsteps of tribal leaders Samsi and Omm-Karja. She may have admired the solo life of the latter, who ran her nomad camp for queen and kids only. Her 20 husbands were never allowed to spend the night; after a quick roll in the tent, back they went to their respective tribes. Zenobia also claimed to hop into bed with her husband only for procreative purposes.

Rather than polyandry, Zenobia hungered for power. Upon her husband's death, she marched into Egypt with an army, took it, and then conquered half of Asia Minor for an encore. Only when she announced Palmyran independence from the Roman Empire did Emperor Aurelian wake up and smell the Arabica coffee. At length he beat Zenobia's forces, but it took him substantial time and resources. Aurelian gained a growing respect for this live-wire queen, who could ride all day and discuss philosophy in three languages over dinner.

Nevertheless, as a victorious general, he wanted a proper homecoming triumph. For the traditional parade of prisoners and exotic beasts, he forced Zenobia to walk through Rome wearing enough golden chains and manacles to sink the Titanic—immediately behind the elephants.

Unsinkable even when ankle-deep in pachyderm dung, Zenobia finessed a life pension for herself instead of the traditional post-triumph slaughter. She even talked Aurelian into providing a villa for her and her sons at Tivoli, the world's first theme park, built by prior emperor Hadrian. On its 750 Disneyesque acres of fantasy architecture and lush landscaped amenities, honeycombed with underground passageways for the service crew slaves, Zenobia lived in honor for some years.

Paraded as Rome's prisoner, Zenobia
kept her cool and cut a deal.

Holier Than Thou
and Richer, Too

When **Melanie the Elder** and her granddaughter, **Melanie the Younger**, flipped from pagan to Christian, they did it big time. Midway through the fourth century, during which Christianity became the official religion of the Roman Empire, Big Mel was one of the richest women in Syria's capital city of Antioch. After joining Antioch's Christian community, the young widow became a disciple of Rufinus, a contemporary of the biblical scholar Jerome. Little Mel, who inherited equal parts Christian fervor and wealth, married her rich cousin, which gave her a fighting chance to outdo Grandma in the "renouncing the material world" giveaway sweepstakes.

Just how much did the Melanies renounce? The Elder Mel owned more than 8,000 slaves, who she freed or sold, giving the money to the church (nice for the church but not quite as satisfactory for the slaves). Little Mel and her husband, who enjoyed an obscene annual income representing millions in current purchasing power, got rid of it all.

The two women also owned whole towns and vast estates in Italy, Spain, Britain, North Africa, and Syria, which they donated for church use. Before Grandma Mel died in A.D. 410, she and her granddaughter threw additional coinage at projects in Egypt, Palestine, Constantinople, and elsewhere, endowing monasteries, feeding the poor, and spiffing up boring church interiors with new silk fabrics and jewels. Although Grandma Mel may have distributed more, granddaughter one-upped her by fast-talking her husband into giving up sex for the rest of their lives. (Let's be fair; she'd had two near-death pregnancies.)

Both generations of Melanies boldly grappled with the theological quarrels that fumed in their day. Big Mel, for example, helped restore unity when church wrangles turned ugly, such as the dispute over what Saint Paul did or didn't mean about the Holy Spirit. That little dustup in Jerusalem involved 400 monks.

After Little Mel's husband died, she settled into a life of prayer, good works, and building a wardrobe of the itchiest ascetic clothing. Haircloth hoods were her favorite. The word about her high piety got around; soon a disgraced royal named **Eudocia** showed up in the Holy Land and wanted to hang out and go relic-collecting.

A century earlier, **Empress Helena** (mom of Constantine and the Holy Land's first tourism booster, which led to the Crusades movement) had made amazing finds. She'd stumbled on nails from the Holy Cross, bones, rags—all of them the holy remnants of saints and apostles—or so she insisted, which turned relic-scrounging into a trend. It's sad to relate, the two souvenir hounds got into a spat. Both Melanie and Eudocia strenuously claimed to have found sacred bits of Saint Stephen the Martyr. The only hitch was they were the same bits.

Altruistic in Any Century

s Jesus had done about 300 years earlier, **Fabiola** focused her attention and love on the overlooked people of her world: the poor, the homeless, the suffering. An offspring of the affluent and distinguished Fabii family of Rome, she converted to Christianity at age 20. Her personal life was messy at first. She married a man so debauched that she was awarded a civil divorce from him. She remarried—an action considered adultery in those times because spouse number one was still alive—which so scandalized her Christian group that they threw her out.

When both men expired, however, the now-respectable widow Fabiola was welcomed back into the fold (after some public penance, of course).

It was a good thing, too, because Fabiola was to do more for public health and Christian kindness than half a hundred of her contemporaries. She first traveled to Bethlehem, planning to join the scholarly monk Jerome and his band of wealthy women activists, who were busy translating the Bible into Latin. Their activities, however, didn't seem lively enough for the gregarious Fabiola. About then the Huns started terrorizing Palestine, promising action of a more dire sort, so Fabiola fled the Holy Land, the translation group right behind her, and returned to Rome.

In Rome's port city of Ostia, with the help of a generous monk named Pammachius, Fabiola established the world's first free public hospital. To carry out the hospital's mission, she recruited a dozen well-to-do Roman matrons to cough up operating funds and to donate time, since compassion, cleanliness, and knowledge of herbs counted for more than official medical training, often sketchy in Fabiola's day. Her facility revolutionized health care, which at that time consisted mostly of military or private care establishments.

A classy lady but far from a delicate flower, Fabiola personally collected patients off the grimy streets of Rome. Jerome was in awe of her unflinching altruism. He called her "the glory of the church, the astonishment of the Gentile, the mother of the poor, and the consolation of the saints." In one of his extant letters, the squeamish monk catalogs some of the suffering folks she rescued: "They have leprous arms, swollen bellies, shrunken thighs, dropsical legs . . . their flesh gnawed and rotten and squirming with little worms."

Besides charity and a strong stomach, this grand woman had energy to spare. She also founded a hospice at Porto Romano that served the area poor as well as sick travelers and

pilgrims. She was busy planning other enterprises when death
caught her by surprise in A.D. 399. All of Rome turned out for
her funeral, especially the humble and grateful people upon
whom she had lavished tender care. A grateful church later
declared Fabiola a saint.

You Think Your Daughter's Boyfriend Is Bad?

o one made a decent likeness of Attila the Hun,
one of the world's truly great bad guys, but we do
have a nice gold coin image of his honey. Unlikely
as it sounds, the Scourge of God had a girlfriend,
Justa Grata Honoria, and she was not just any
lowlife Hun-happy hot mama, either. Justa was the sister of
Valentinian III, emperor of the western half of the Roman
Empire.

Justa may have been just a tad high-spirited. Allegedly
devoted to Christian celibacy, she got a wee bit knocked up in
A.D. 434. Attila wasn't in the picture yet; the proud father was a
commoner. Since everyone at the imperial court thought Justa
planned a run at the emperorship, brother Val grounded his sister,
banishing her to the care of a family member in Constantinople.
For good measure, he gave Justa's co-conspirator—and possibly
the baby—a permanent time-out. When Justa was finally allowed
to return to Italy, Valentinian signed her up to marry a pedigreed
fellow with no tiresome ambitions.

Wily Justa had her own game plan. Her brother hadn't executed all of her personal servants yet, which enabled her to send her eunuch Hyacinth to the camp of Attila the Hun, who was currently chewing on the weakening edges of the Roman Empire. The eunuch carried Justa's ring and a mushy note, saying how fabulous she thought he was, and would he be interested in a coup for two—for a generous fee, naturally. An old romantic at heart, Attila fired back an okay and an offer of marriage (with the understanding that her dowry would be the western half of the Roman Empire, of course). Inevitably, brother Val got wind of it and tried to break up the pen-pals by telling Attila: "My sister's taken! And besides, she doesn't have any rights to the throne—so get lost."

Never a barbarian to take "Hell, no!" for an answer, Attila invaded Gaul to show his feelings, later showing up to lay waste to Italy and claim his unlikely fiancée. Since Italy lacked a SWAT team at that time, Pope Leo jumped in to negotiate with the number-one Hun and keep him from burning Rome to the ground.

Providence only knows what might have happened if spitfire Justa had been able to gallop off with Attila. But malign fate (and Attila's wandering eye) intervened. In 453, before this odd couple could build a relationship or even wreak a little revenge, Attila died. The cause? A fatal nosebleed that hit him during his over-enthusiastic wedding feast to another eager chick.

PART TWO

UPPITY WOMEN

OF

Medieval Times

ca. A.D. 450–1450

Don't Cry for Me, Byzantinos

In the bustle and hype of sixth-century Constantinople, you had to be outrageous to get noticed. Freakishness was a breeze for **Theodora**, whose beauty and talent for exhibitionism let her develop an act that combined porn, dried corn, carefully trained geese, and her next-to-naked body in a hide-and-go-seek performance that had Byzantines gasping. A great actress and comic dancer, this petite forerunner of Evita Perón soon got the hottest parts going in the pantomime theater, an entertainment that combined the erotic, the vulgar, and the horrifying as cleverly as Theodora did.

This slum child got into showbiz early. Her father, an animal trainer at the hippodrome racetrack, did a disappearing act when she was a tot. Her mom, burdened with three daughters, encouraged them to dance, show a little thigh, and bring home the bacon. Before puberty ever arrived at Thea's door, she had to do some very grown-up sinning as a child prostitute.

After a stint as somebody's mistress and a stay in Alexandria, Egypt, she returned to Constantinople a neophyte Christian—which was fortunate, because soon thereafter she met devout emperor-in-waiting Justinian. Besides religion, the pair shared an interest in Thea's physical equipment. But she also possessed something even more shocking than her inventive porn work—a top-notch intelligence. About A.D. 525 (after Justinian passed a law allowing him to wed an actress), she and he got married, to shock and envy all around.

Like other women with checkered pasts, Theodora put hers behind her once married. The new empress immediately got a makeover: a gold-coin-adorned crown for height, a long white dress with purple cloak, and a heavily jeweled bib and tucker. The power dressing was just for image, however. She also brought sensible advice, political acumen, and courage to her position.

During the Blue and Green riots, fomented by crazed chariot-racing fans turned political rebels, for instance, Justinian panicked and wanted to flee when his troops couldn't control the situation. Theodora said: "You want to *what*? We're all gonna die anyway—might as well do it wearing the purple." Her scathing remarks, and her tactical help in quelling the riots, got Justinian back into command mode. Remotivated troops then made shish kebab out of 30,000 rioters, who had by this point burned down most of Constantinople.

One good thing about smoking ruins—they leave plenty of opportunities to put up some really decent new buildings. With Thea's help, the emperor's builders set to work; some of their efforts, such as the Cathedral of Santa Sophia (the Hagia Sophia mosque today) and fragments of its stunning mosaics, are still around.

In 542, the dynamic duo's reign was tested by an even bigger disaster: plague. Killing as many as 10,000 people a day, it decimated the city. It tapped Justinian on the shoulder, but he didn't dare die—his stalwart nurse Thea would be so cross. They both survived the epidemic, only to have Theodora contract cancer at age 40. At her death, she left behind a grieving husband and empire—a final exit that would be eerily echoed by the life of actress-turned-"empress" Evita Perón, 1,400 years later.

Mother Knows Best

On October 19, A.D. 612, a mysterious noblewoman called **Zac-Kuk** (Sak K'uk' on some inscriptions) took the throne of B'aakal and its capital, Lakamha, the site of Palenque, Mexico, today. Her name meant "resplendent quetzal." Like any fashion-conscious Mayan of her day, she had crossed eyes, jade-inlaid teeth, and a sloping forehead to accentuate her resplendent nose.

Once powerful, her domain was in a bad way; archaeologists now know that after eight years of military disasters, the capital had been viciously sacked by enemies in 611, who also killed the ruler and heir, both males. For three years, Queen Zac-Kuk held things together from the mural-bright palace. When her son and male heir, Pacal, turned 12 and stopped playing *pok-a-tok*, the Mayan version of hoops, Zac-Kuk evidently decided he was ready enough. In exquisitely carved scenes on an archaeological

Zac-Kuk's son, Pacal, made Palenque a beautiful city again, with his mother's help.

find known as the Oval Palace Tablet we can see the moment on July 26, 615, when Zac-Kuk handed over the royal headdress to her son.

Not one to let a teen work without supervision, she (assisted by her consort) kept a grip until Pacal got the hang of ruling. She remained influential for decades, encouraging her son to revive the arts, remodel the palace, and rebuild the city. He did so, becoming known as Pacal the Great. We don't know nearly as much as we'd like to about Zac-Kuk, but thanks to the ancient Mayan obsession with numbers, we have the precise date of her death: September 12, 640.

Super Ks Charm Japan

 lthough being a Buddhist nun had kept her in a nonstop whirl of meditation and temple construction, Princess **Koken** finally agreed to become empress of Japan in 749, when her abdicating dad said, "You gotta help me out here."

For 20 years, she and her mom, **Komyo,** had been on a building spree. With the emperor's help, they'd established temples and nunneries throughout Japan—and made their capital city of Nara a religious center. Buddhism, it was thought, would also keep natural disasters at bay. Nobody wanted a replay of 644, when a terrible famine led survivors to start a new religion, based on street dancing and drinking lots of sake, whose supreme being was a giant worm.

More recently, Koken and family had lived through a small-pox epidemic that had wiped out many nobles in the Japanese court. Koken felt she hadn't done quite enough for Buddhism yet. So the brand-new empress hired 116 priests as demon-busters; completed the world's biggest bronze and goldleaf

Buddha statue; and made the chief priest, Dokyo, an administration czar. Dokyo, a medieval Dr. Feel-good, was Koken's
personal physician, who had shot to the top of the esteem chart
by curing her of an unspecified ailment.

As the energetic empress brainstormed further, she came
across a religious text that said you could be cured of disease and
lengthen your life if you placed a certain number of written
charms in the nearest temple. Excited, Empress Koken ordered
up a nice round number: one *million* charms. Japan already had
the technology of block printing; even so, her friendly neighborhood printer was stunned by the order. Each charm had 25 lines
of holy words encased in a wooden pagoda five inches high.
Naturally the empress wanted it yesterday; even with people on
overtime, however, she didn't get her complete plague-evading
print run until 770.

Temples throughout Japan were promptly awash in pagoda
charms, and Empress Koken was just getting compliments on
her idea when another smallpox epidemic struck. And wouldn't
you know it, Buddha (or perhaps that scary giant worm) had the
last laugh: Fifty-two-year-old Koken was one of its victims.

Some of her charms, however, are still hanging around—the
earliest examples ever found of copper block printing. Several
temples built by this devout mom-and-daughter tag team still
stand in Nara, Japan. And that mon-
ster statue of Buddha? No longer
the world's biggest, it still graces
Nara's Todai-ji temple.

Sufi Miracle Worker

icknamed "that woman on fire with love," **Rabi'a al-Adawiya** was not, as you might first think, a courtesan or a much-wed Baghdad starlet. Rather, she was a pivotal figure in the early development of Sufism, which is to Islam what mysticism is to Christianity. An ethical sect that renounced worldly comforts and embraced blissful union with a supreme being, Sufism also used music and dance as a path to spiritual ecstasy.

Born in 717, about a century after Muhammad the Prophet's death, Rabi'a sprang from a humble family, rich only in daughters. Poverty was tough enough, but a terrible famine hit the city of Basra, the family got separated, and Rabi'a ended up on the streets. Before long, a man who made a living from orphans' misfortunes sold her as a household slave.

Despite her hard life, Rabi'a had a strong contemplative bent. When her work was finished, she would stand in prayer until dawn. One night, her owner caught her contemplating so hard that a shining lamp appeared to be levitating over her head. Thoroughly spooked, he freed her immediately.

Rabi'a left her Persian Gulf port city of Basra and headed for a hermitage in the desert, where she could become a religious recluse and pursue celibacy and enlightenment in peace and quiet. Although unlettered, Rabi'a became a teacher and scholar, as famous for her Sufi sayings in prose and poetry as for her exemplary life. Once the word got around, the mystic started attracting fans, followers, and suitors. Hoping for a spirituality shortcut, rich new friends offered her money. When others pushed her to take it, she said, "I'd truly be ashamed to ask for worldly things from Him to whom the world belongs; so why would I ask for the same things from those to whom it does not belong?"

At another point in her life, Rabi'a set out to make her pilgrimage to the Islamic holy city of Mecca, nearly a thousand
miles south and west of her simple quarters in the Iraqi desert.
In mid-desert, her donkey died. Rabi'a, alone and stumped,
began to pray to God for help. Her powers of prayer were such,
it was said, that the donkey came back to life—
whereupon the holy woman jumped on and
continued her pilgrimage.

Unlike her Muslim contemporaries, she
wasn't obsessed with heaven and hell. Rabi'a's
commitment to divine love, her simple
and loving doctrine, made her one of
Sufi's earliest high authorities. She lived
to be 80, a grand old woman later credited
with many miraculous feats, from communi-
cating with animals to making prayer rugs fly. Even
without the miracles, her life bears witness to the spiritual
stature even the humblest women sometimes attained. Poet and
Sufi mystic Omar Khayyam may have been more famous, but
Rabi'a reached a level of dignity and respect as holy as that given
to any of the male mystics of Islam.

An Early Islamic Asset

In eighth-century Iraq, Harun al-Rashid, known to us as
Aaron the Upright, knew a good thing when he saw it:
his kissin' cousin **Zubaidah**, whom he promptly made
his wife. When Aaron became caliph of Baghdad,
Zubaidah put together an Arabian court whose style would be
captured in fiction a century later in *The Book of One Thousand
and One Nights*. A glamour guru, she presided in jewel-studded
shoes, served rareties such as iced melon delivered (on foot, of

course) from Persia, and staged cast-of-thousands extravaganzas
and floating concerts on the Tigris River.

Zubaidah also kept a few coins tucked under her magic carpet
for worthy purposes. She repaired roads, dug roadside wells, established reservoirs, and put up hostels—all to improve the 900-mile
pilgrim route between Baghdad and the holy city
of Mecca in Arabia. Then as now, every
devout Muslim sought to visit Mecca,
the pilgrimage or *hajj* being one of
the five tenets of Islam. Zubaidah's
husband made the pilgrimage
every other year—on foot—so
she had him in mind as well. Ever
after, the route was called Zubaidah's
Way in remembrance.

In due time, her own son,
Muhammad al-Amin, became caliph. Fond
mom had barely picked out her swearing-in
outfit when he was murdered in a succession battle.
Generous-minded to the last, Zubaidah refused to avenge her
son's killing; in so doing, she kept her land from civil war. This
lovely blossom died in A.D. 831 and was buried in a tomb that
resembles a flower.

Saxon Overachiever

n the ninth century, folks called weaving maven **Liutbirg**
of Germany a miracle worker—and meant it in every
sense of the word. Clothmaking was the industry to
watch in Europe; after centuries of feudal no-growth, a
retail renaissance was turning fortress-cities into urban centers.

Most clothmaking, finishing, and dyeing was done in women's workshops, such as the good-sized one run by Liutbirg, a humble Saxon servant of German countess Gisla and her son. These two knew an overachiever when they saw one. After honeyed words from her employers, loyal Liutbirg took on more chores: nursing the sick, administering the affairs of the palace, even running a swing-shift school for girls to teach them weaving, spinning, needlework, reading, psalm-singing, and cloth dyeing. At retirement, instead of asking for a putting green or entertainment center in her unplush quarters, Liutbirg requested a tiny prayer cell and a coal furnace, so she could continue to worship God, dye cloth, and teach the craft. Is it any wonder this Saxon perpetual motion machine got tapped for sainthood down the line?

If you ask me, the new 80-hour work week seems sinfully decadent.

Unsinkable Viking Granny

Aud the Deep-Minded was a new breed of Viking—a kinder, gentler Norsewoman. After centuries of pillaging, piracy, and property snatching, her brand of behavior was more than welcome.

Born in 855, Aud grew up in the Scottish islands of the Hebrides, getting her spiritual depth from her mother, a Celtic

Christian, and her direction-finding ability from dad, Ketil Flatnose, a Norwegian Viking. After a brief spin at matrimony to a Dublin king named Olaf the White, the new divorcée and her son, Thorstein the Red, enjoyed several decades of peacefully micromanaging the Hebrides. Aud was busy spoiling her grand-children and doing a little contemplation when along came a couple of Scots who hadn't gotten the word that mayhem was officially over, and killed Aud's son.

Opting to flee rather than fight, Aud built a ship, loaded it with big denomination currency, jammed her grandchildren and a band of followers on board, and hauled keel outta there. First she island-hopped to the Orkneys, where she married off a granddaughter to the local chief; then to the Faroes, where she did ditto. While scenic, both places seemed way too cramped for a gal who was used to something more in the 2,900-square-mile range.

Aud's two brothers were already in a place with the unpromising name of Iceland. When the Deep-Minded one heard the details, however, she shooed everyone back on the ship and set off. Some 300 horribly seasick miles across the North Atlantic Ocean, Aud and company spotted an ample chunk of land. Before she could even announce, "We're here!" the ship hit a reef and sank, giving everyone a chance to see just how cool Iceland's waters were. (Thankfully, most on board had swimming or timber-clinging skills.)

On shore, a bedraggled Aud counted heads. The grandkids made it, as did some 20 faithful followers, a number of slaves, and most of grandma's treasures, now a soggy mass of flotsam and jetsam.

If you thought that shipwreck was a cold experience, you

should have seen the welcome Aud's brother Helgi gave them. One look, and he said, "Only room for ten of the least squishy." Aud steamed off to her other brother's, who was wise enough not to push his luck with the kinder, gentler Viking idea.

Once dry, our senior explorer borrowed a boat and began circling Iceland, examining the deeply indented coast, and setting a bonfire wherever she saw some property she fancied to officially stake her claim. At the end of her shopping trip, Aud had claimed about 180 square miles.

Now it was divvying up time—and grandma had a ball. Followers, grandkids, and slaves got huge parcels, marked with Christian crosses. One granddaughter got an entire river valley as a dowry; Aud sprang for the wedding besides. As her final official act, Grandma Deep choreographed the marriage of her youngest grandson. At the reception, she greeted the guests, made sure the ale was flowing—and then went off to her eternal rest. At her request, this best and brightest of the Viking matriarchs was buried on Iceland's coast, in the salty land below the high-water mark.

Aethelfled's War and Peace Program

For an aggressive ninth-century Anglo-Saxon like Aethelfled, England was a paradise of pugnacity. She and her husband, Ethelred, often worked together on the battlefield. Like her daddy, Alfred the Great, she relished the warrior role, which certainly beat that whole pregnancy business. Granted, she enjoyed having daughter Aelfwyn around but Aethelfled still shuddered when

remembering labor pains. Luckily there was no shortage of battles to attend, which kept conjugal demands to a minimum.

At that time, England was a snarl of small quarreling kingdoms—and outsider attacks were frequent. Aethelfled's father
had spent his life fighting the Danes, who considered England
"the Viking destination we'd most like to pillage and burn."

After both her dad and her husband died, Aethelfled spent
eight years building fortresses, leading troops into Wales, and
helping her brother Edward out militarily. After she got the
quarreling Mercians of central England to accept unity, however,
Aethelfled saw the light—and got the equally prickly Brits,
Picts, and Scots to unite against the Danish Vikings.

Aethelfled came to be looked on as unofficial ruler of
England. Due to the success of her warrior/negotiator approach,
everyone expected her daughter to follow her. Sure enough, in
918 when Aethelfled caught the wrong end of a mace in a battle at Stratfordshire, Aelfwyn inherited the crown. About ten
minutes later, however, her Uncle Edward "forgot" about the
years of military aid his sister had given him, pushed Aelfwyn
aside, and made himself king of England.

Trio of Holy Terrors

ussian history includes female rulers who were by
turns brutal, bold, and bawdy—and sometimes
all three.

Around A.D. 945 a dynamo named **Queen
Olga** was having a dickens of a time. A Slavic
tribe had just killed her husband, King Igor. As new ruler, she
methodically went after the guilty parties, wiping them out in

ways designed to put the fear of Olga into the survivors. The first batch of 20 she buried alive; she parboiled the second batch inside their bathhouses. After that she hosted a massacre of 5,000, relying on more conventional sword-stabbing. By now her subjects were quite ready to pay annual tribute and let Olga reign. When she introduced the Greek Orthodox form of Christianity to Russia, peasants and aristocrats alike bought into it, no questions asked. For her outstanding slaughter-for-God work, she was declared a saint—one of only five women to ever win the halo from the Orthodox Church.

Called Catherine the Great by her subjects—and her lovers.

Two centuries later, 22-year-old **Queen Tamar** co-ruled Russian Georgia, some beautifully wild real estate wedged between the Black and Caspian seas. She and her father, George, had a nice tandem act; as monarch in training, Tamar got copious hints from George about running a country, squelching rebels, and all that.

Also an enthusiastic Christian, Tamar lusted to possess the best icon money could buy—that would be a piece of the true cross, of course. She'd heard that Saladin, the Arab leader who'd taken Jerusalem by whipping the crusaders, had a chunk. Tamar offered him 200,000 gold pieces for it; Saladin snubbed her. Disgruntled, she returned to unabashed military expansion of Georgia and ushering in her country's golden age. Those gold coins of her must have been spectacular—and huge, since they bore some of her many titles: King of Kings, Queen of Queens, Glory of the World and Faith, and Champion of the Messiah.

That brings us to **Catherine the Great,** empress of Russia, who was a champion at both ruling and eroticism. A native of Prussia selected as the 15-year-old fiancée to Peter III, heir to the Russian throne, she became much more of a Russian—and a ruler—than he. (That wasn't hard, since Peter was a wizened, nasty brute of a fellow.)

Six months after becoming tsar, Peter lost his throne and key body parts in an (almost) bloodless coup that installed Catherine as empress. The energetic new ruler added 200,000 square miles to Russia. All that warlike activity made her hungry, so to speak. Thus, she regularly indulged in a spectacular series of young male lovers, many of whom became her most trusted ministers and on whom she spent an estimated 12 million pounds during her 34-year reign.

Apocalypse, Spanish Style

 aking advantage of the great interest in gloom, doom, and matters millennial, around 970 a Spanish painter named **Ende** created a highly imaginative series on the Apocalypse in book form. In Ende's day, the Catholic Church was the only game in town so far as the production and illustration (called illumination) of sacred texts. We know little about the artist, other than that she was a nun and a woman of the upper classes. Ende had a very Spanish talent; the flowing lines, playful stars, semicomic dragons, and bands of color in her work transcend time to produce an effect more Joan Miró than Middle Age. A woman who gave credit where credit was due, she signed her work "Ende painter and (with) the help of God and Brother Emeterius

Presbyter." The monk who served as her assistant has a style identified from another signed manuscript; scholars are confident that most of the Gerona Apocalypse illuminations are the work of Ende—and her supreme inspiration. Ende's artful manuscript, in what is today called the Mozarabic style, can still be admired at the cathedral in Gerona, Spain, where she painted it.

Gerona, hometown of mystical artist Ende.

Hymen Repair, Our Specialty

he doctor who dazzled the Dark Ages, **Trotula** studied and later practiced medicine during the 11th century at Salerno, Italy's famed medical school—the first of its kind in medieval Europe. Doctoring ran in her family. This bright Neapolitan woman married a sawbones named John Platearius; their sons Matteo and John went on to make it a doctor dynasty. Around the breakfast table, she might have been called "*mamma mía*," but elsewhere, even her sons referred to her as "Dr. Platearii" or "learned mother Trocta." Son Matteo was careful to point out in writing that his mom was a *magistra*, or university-trained doctor, not merely an *empiric*, or midwife.

Trotula made the study of women her specialty; among her good deeds, she pioneered surgical techniques for repair of the perineum, a critical piece of female anatomy often damaged in childbirth, as any postpartum mother with an aching backside knows. Trotula also wrote two important medical books: *The Diseases of Women*, often referred to as *Trotula Major*, covered obstetrics, gynecology, and general medicine; the second, *Trotula Minor*, dealt with skin treatments. More than 100 manuscript copies of her writings still exist—and her work was consulted and plagiarized for centuries.

Much of her advice remains valid. For instance, the good doctor advocated the use of opiates to ease childbirth pain and prescribed hormonal treatments (made from animal testicles) to regulate menstruation and overcome sterility. She also was very big on cleanliness—its lack being a leading cause of mother and infant death until the 20th century.

Not all of Dr. T's medical palaver was so high-minded,

however. Her most popular contributions may be the ones she made to the state of virginity. In medieval times, as now, young virgins sometimes turned into young, hot-to-trot vixens. Once they had trotted, so to speak, the delicate issue of their modified equipment became priority number one when they got engaged. For her maidenhead-obsessed age, the ingenious physician invented a number of remedies for making former virgins almost as good as new—if not as good as gold.

Dr. T's most useful prescription called for putting a leech on the area in question the day before the wedding. Although medieval folks thought nothing of slapping on a leech or two for a quick bleeding (their equivalent of two aspirin), the make-a-virgin procedure was trickier. Keeping track of the darned thing (leeches move fast) was key. Revirginal candidates also had to make sure they removed the bloodthirsty little critters before they got too many quarts low—as Dr. Trotula would second, a corpselike pallor makes it tough to be a radiant bride.

Poetry by the Camel Load

 n 11th-century "I did it my way" poet, **Wallada al-Mustakfi** trashed the conventional rules of what a noble Moorish girl in Andalusian Spain should and shouldn't do. She lived in tumultuous times, when the caliph rulers of Córdoba took turns assassinating each other. After her dad, a rascally fellow named Muhammad III, bit the dust, Wallada inherited his properties—and promptly turned his palace into a literary salon for poets and intellectuals of her day.

Wallada, whose talents extended to teacher as well as poet

and singer, presided over a brilliant circle. At the circle's gatherings, writers vied to see who could most eloquently complete an unfinished verse, a contest Wallada often won.

Women of her era dutifully wore veils; Wallada laughed at that notion. Instead, she wore garments lavishly embroidered with provocative lines, such as, "I feel free to give my kisses to whomever asks for them."

Wallada's kisses did get rather wide distribution among her lovers, male and female. She and nobleman Ibn Zaydún met at a poetry slam and later shared their passions. They kept their long-distance romance under wraps because—as with Romeo and Juliet—their tribes were rivals. Although the couple split up, nine of Wallada's poems survive from the camel-loads of poetic correspondence they exchanged.

Wallada was also linked romantically with students, including Muhya al-Tayyani, a young woman she mentored. In the face of such free-spirited behavior, Andalusians predicted dire

*Now called La Mesquita, Córdoba's lovely mosque
was a familiar landmark to Wallada.*

things for this woman. To their disgust, none materialized. Later in Wallada's life, a high-ranking official fell for her and cosseted her until they both expired as happy octogenarians.

Envious Eyewitness

royal whiz kid who lived in the beautiful Byzantine city of Constantinople at the time of the First Crusade, **Anna Comnena** became a writer and wrote on psychosomatic disease. Among her examples was the connection she saw between envy and gangrene. Envy is too pale a word for the lifelong resentment she felt—and wrote about endlessly.

Here's why: *Porphyrogenitus,* or "born to the purple," Princess Anna got engaged at the tender age of eight to the heir apparent. Clear sailing it would seem—until along came that horror of medieval times, a royal baby brother, who was replacing her honey as the heir. Worse yet, Anna's young husband-to-be died, leaving her a nine-year-old fiancée in mourning.

Meanwhile, Anna's father, Emperor Alexius, who saw that his beloved daughter was no slouch in the brains department, made sure she got a brilliant education, studying astronomy, medicine, history, military affairs, music, geography, math, and literature from the holy scriptures to the classical authors. This learning was to serve Anna well.

In 1096, the First Crusade, which flooded Constantinople with thousands of armed troops, freelance fanatics, and unarmed pilgrims, brought with it an urgent need for expanded medical facilities. The emperor built a 10,000-bed hospital/orphanage; Anna became its administrator. (Some claim she got in a little hands-on doctoring as well.) Because daddy suffered from gout, she began studying and writing on medical matters.

Knights in shining armor, they weren't. Knights in mud- and blood-spattered armor is more like it.

The princess didn't know it then, but she would most be remembered for her book, *The Alexiad.* Besides lavishing praise on her pop, Anna's still-in-print book covered the comings and goings of the crusaders (or "Franks" as the Byzantines called them). It's the only female eyewitness account we still have of those tumultuous events. Her words make us realize that the Crusades weren't just a guy thing: "Full of ardor and enthusiasm, they thronged every highway; and with these warriors came a host of civilians, outnumbering the grains of sand on the seashore, carrying palms [palm fronds] in their hands and bearing crosses on their shoulders. There were women and children too, who had left their own countries. Like tributaries joining a river, they streamed from all directions toward us."

Author Comnena unblinkingly reported on everything from the tactical use of flamethrowers on her father's ships to the atrocities (including baby roasting and cannibalism) reportedly committed by the crusaders when they recaptured the city of Nicaea for good ole Byzantium.

Despite her considerable achievements, Anna felt cheated and kept trying to become empress one way or another. Although she improved her position in the next-of-kin sweepstakes by marrying and producing two sons, she never got into the semifinals with dad. She wasn't a quitter, however. Even after her father's death in 1118, she tried every trick in the book to grab the throne for her spouse—including two conspiracies to put her brother, the brand-new emperor, on ice permanently.

Busted for her role in the would-be coups, Anna grumped all the way into the convent, where she had (every writer's fantasy!) the next 35 years to polish her manuscript and her most vicious *bons mots* at leisure.

From her city's walls, Anna saw and wrote about
the civilians involved in the First Crusade.

A Millennial in a Million

fter a mock funeral ceremony, her parents said a final *"Auf Wiedersehen"* and locked eight-year-old **Hildegard of Bingen** into a cell with the dimensions and comforts of a walk-in freezer. Was she a plague victim? Hopelessly insane? A budding young criminal of the Middle Ages? Believe it or not, incarceration as an anchorite or anchoress was chosen by many children and/or their parents. By 1098, when Hildegard was born in the Rhine district of Germany, there were countless kids in religious lockup. Unlike nuns, anchorites were required to stay in their cells until death.

A frail youngster, Hildegard had religious visions; her aristocratic parents decided to tithe her to God, placing her in a one-room, one-windowed enclosure at the Disibodenburg monastic order. This meager space was already occupied by Jutta, an anchoress lifer who taught the girl reading, writing, Latin, and music. Other than trips to the privy, Hildegard spent the next seven years in the lockbox.

By degrees, word spread about the child's extraordinary spiritual and intellectual gifts; other women who wished to study with her jammed into the space, which eventually turned her semisolitary confinement into—a nunnery. Sensing the contradiction, the powers that be commuted her solitary confinement into nun status (which also gave Hildegard a chance to see the rest of the monastery).

In her serene surroundings, Hildegard had ample time to develop the talents God had bestowed. More than 200 years before the Renaissance was dreamed of, this woman displayed prodigious abilities as religious mystic, writer, composer, playwright, healer, artist, botanist, and administrator.

After Jutta died, Hildegard was elected to head up the fledgling group of nuns. Her experiences running the convent—and later moving to new quarters and establishing a second convent on the Rhine—gradually turned her from a highly diffident person into a more self-assured woman.

When Hildegard turned 42, she had a vision that was decisive in her transformation from contemplative to activist. About it, she said, "A blinding light of exceptional brilliance flowed through my entire brain. And so it kindled my whole heart and breast like a flame, not burning but warming . . . and suddenly I was able to taste of the understanding of books." (Her visions are now thought to have been triggered by migraine; what sets her apart from other migraine sufferers is what she accomplished as a result of her illness.)

Hildegard had colorful visions that were turned into mystical works of art.

The writings from her unfettered mind included mystery plays, an opera, poems, and books. Their subject matter ranged from theology to natural history to healing. Among Hildegard's herbal tips: Mandrake root would ease depression and love-sickness; camphor was useful for keeping nuns alert during Mass. She described 485 herbs and plants, and her words on hops were the first written reference to them in beer-making.

For a sheltered virgin, Hildegard had some pretty frank things to say about sex—including what may be the first written description of the female orgasm. In our day, her musical legacy is getting equal attention from New Age and early music fans.

Female mystics were a dime a dozen in medieval times.

Hildegard's prophetic message to the world, however, centered around the goodness of creation and God's pleasure in it. Naturally this upset the fire-and-brimstoners. To the end of her very long life, Hildegard fought for a tolerant, just, and positive spirituality in a European world echoing with an often hateful and narrow Christianity.

Artful Bamboo Artists

While Mongol hordes were busy conquering China in the 12th and 13th centuries, **Kuan Tao-sheng** was busy taking the country by storm with her delicate bamboo paintings and calligraphy.

This popular genre had been invented during the turbulent Five Dynasties period of the tenth century by another woman, Szechuan calligrapher **Li Fu-jen**. Accounts differ as to whether Li Fu-jen was imprisoned in an isolated house or she simply happened to suffer from insomnia. One sleepless moonlit night, staring at her rice-paper window, she saw the eloquent, moving shadows made by the bamboo leaves outside. They reminded her of calligraphy—so she grabbed a brush and began to trace the shapes on her window.

Kuan Tao-sheng probably had some sleepless nights as well—because she became the mother of nine. Her husband, Chao, an artist and calligrapher himself, was supportive of his wife's gifts; at times they collaborated artistically and personally. When he became a high-level secretary for Kublai Khan, his wife accompanied him everywhere on official trips around China—a most unusual activity for a wife in those days. (Concubines on trips, yes; wives, never the norm.)

As she developed, Kuan mastered all four forms of Chinese painting, from hand scrolls to wall paintings. Her style, an eye-pleasing minimal approach, featured bamboos in all seasons and weather. Many of her pieces, including *Bamboo Groves in Mist and Rain* (now in Taipei's National Palace Museum) can still be marveled at.

During Kuan's lifetime, the Khan administration, anxious to shake its barbarian conquerer image, became an active patron of culture. According to her husband's memoirs, Kuan received kudos on all sides and "imperial favors as abundant as rains." Some of that admiring downpour may even have come from a westerner named Marco Polo, a nearly permanent houseguest of Kublai Khan.

Kuan Tao-sheng also wrote a treatise on painting before she died in 1319 of beri-beri, a wasting disease caused by lack of vitamin B_1.

Courtly Lives,
Relived in Print

ife was rugged in medieval Japan for women like **Lady Nijo** and **Lady Murasaki**. There was the daily grind of sake parties; the relentless ritual of selecting the absolutely right seven-layer silk gown to match the day and season from one's huge wardrobe; and the nonstop chores of writing a hand-calligraphed poem for every occasion, from the most fleeting of meetings to the most minor thank-you. These exquisite activities (and others not nearly so exquisite) absorbed Japan's aristocrats for centuries.

We think *we* live in a nostalgia-crazy society—Lady Nijo (born in 1257) and her sensitive pals based their entire lives on the actions, words, and behavior from a novel written in 1008 by another Japanese high-society woman!

Known only by the name of her heroine, Lady Murasaki, the author called her 54-volume masterpiece *The Tale of Genji*. Although heavily fictionalized, *Genji* was based on Murasaki's own years of service to Empress Akiko, to whom she taught Chinese literature on the sly. The mystery author also kept a diary of court life, its raw material eventually becoming her novel about Prince Genji and his loves. With this feat, this unknown Japanese genius created the world's earliest novel. A talented bilingual artist, she also wrote poetry in Japanese and Chinese.

Two centuries after Murasaki, a small 14-year-old was given as a bed-toy to a Japanese emperor with the provocative name of GoFukasaka. The unwilling young concubine eventually became a compliant courtesan named Lady Nijo (Lady Second Avenue)—and an observer of court life whose acuity of vision and wit were the equal of earlier writer Murasaki.

In between love affairs and a child or two, Nijo also started a diary. After 12 years at court, this fun-loving social climber was expelled over some extra-curricular activity with old GoFukasaka's brother and political rival. Still a woman of great personal charm and talents in music, poetry, and painting, Lady Nijo shaved her head, gave up (with a wince perhaps) those gorgeous silk garments, and became a Buddhist nun.

In many respects, her book, a delicately acid and funny tell-all called *The Confessions of Lady Nijo*, echoes Lady Murasaki's masterpiece. Like one of those marvelous oriental nested boxes, her story contains both her own poetry and echoes of the Heian culture of Murasaki that Nijo and her friends strove so hard to emulate.

There was one important difference between these two giants of Japanese literature, however: Nijo's book was nonfiction. In describing court capers, she used the real names of the all-too-human emperor and his family. That's why the book remained underground for more than six centuries. In 1940, a scholar stumbled across the only existing copy, disguised as a treatise on geography. Besides their value as history and litera-ture, the works of Ladies Nijo and Murasaki reveal a universality of female experience that is startlingly contemporary.

Platonic Friends, the Hard Way

masculating women? The Dark Ages had 'em. But in **Heloise**'s case, the emasculation was totally unintentional. *Her* hints from Heloise would have read: "If you jump into bed with a clergyman, never get pregnant. And forget about telling your relatives!"

At age 17, this bright young Parisian intellectual began studying philosophy with Peter Abelard, twice her age and the hottest celebrity theologist in 12th-century France. Pete's tutoring quickly turned into something more earthy, unwittingly aided by Heloise's clergyman uncle, who naïvely rented him a room in their house.

There was a flaming row when Uncle Fulbert found out about the sex—and a worse one when Heloise turned up preg-gers. After she gave birth to a son named (shades of the 60s!) Astrolabe, Pete promised the uncle he'd marry Heloise if it could be kept secret; a calculating sort, Abelard didn't want to jeopar-dize his sunny career possibilities in the church.

At this juncture, however, a major failure to communicate took place. Abelard took Heloise to the convent where she'd been educated, ostensibly to hide out until their wedding, where the lovebirds did more than a little aardvarking in a quiet corner of the refectory.

It's not clear whether the two actually married or not. What is clear is that fond uncle got the notion that Mr. Hot-cassock was abandoning or disgracing his niece. (And maybe he was.) At any rate, Uncle Fulbert took action. He hired a couple of dagger-equipped suits, who broke into Pete's room one night and castrated him.

The horrified lovers immediately joined his-and-her religious orders. (Actually, Abelard leaned on Heloise to join up and waited until she did before entering a monastery.) Peter did stints at several monasteries, becoming a scholarly monk whose teachings continued to irk the church—and finally got himself denounced as a heretic. For her part, Heloise reluctantly embraced nunhood, eventually becoming abbess of Paraclete convent, founded by Peter in 1129.

Although nothing else could smolder, their correspondence went on hot and heavy for years. Despite its contradictions, the Heloise and Abelard romance became one of the most-repeated stories of their age and later centuries. The first letter Heloise wrote to Abelard said, in part: "I was more pleased with possessing your heart than with any other happiness . . . the man was the thing I least valued in you."

Judging by the intelligence and fire displayed in her eloquent letters, Heloise deserved better than a self-righteous and randy religious man. Chemistry is chemistry, however, even when you cover it with a habit. Her passion for Pete burned unabated throughout her life, and she was buried by his side, 20 years after his death.

From one of Heloise's letters to Abelard: "I ought to deplore what we did—but I sigh only for what we have lost."

The World Was Eleanor's Canvas

hrowing on some low-cut gilded armor, rounding up a few thousand vassals and a couple of high-society girlfriends in matching outfits, and riding off to the Crusades was just another lark for **Eleanor of Aquitaine**, easily the most glamorous household name around Europe in the 12th century. Even given the fact she lived to be 83, she crammed in an amazing amount of accomplishment and adventure.

To start with, she ruled as queen of France for 15 years and queen of England for 50 more, producing ten kids when she wasn't busy with music, health care, or political maneuverings.

A jet-setter 900 years before jets, Eleanor couldn't do just one thing at a time. While making her way to Jerusalem with husband King Louis on the Second Crusade, for instance, she noticed the carnage en route and founded a few hospitals to help out. That done, they moved on to Antioch, where Eleanor flirted with her Uncle Raymond and other fun-loving royals of Syria. Damp-blanket Louie, meanwhile, shaved off his hair and beard—which moved the queen to say, "That chin is grounds for a divorce." Their marriage, which had produced two daughters, was eventually annulled; the Second Crusade, a major embarrassment despite Eleanor's contributions, *should* have been annulled also.

Now 30, the new divorcée quickly wed 19-year-old Henry II, soon to be king of England. Was it real love this time? More like real *estate*: Their combined holdings included England and more than half of France—which really put a certain ex-husband's nose out of joint, as did Eleanor's ability to produce male heirs with Henry. Soon there were eight little Plantagenets running around.

This marriage turned out to be no bed of roses either, as Eleanor watched Henry get fatter and more faithless.

In 1170, royally fed up with the philandering Plantagenet, Eleanor and her daughter Marie turned their courts in France and England into troubadour-filled "courts of love," built around the premise that "true love is a game for single people."

Passion might be fun and games, but Eleanor evidently found politics and war games more to her liking. At age 50, she and two of her sons led her Aquitaine army against Henry. The king took it in double overtime and left the queen to spend her next 15 years under house arrest in one drafty castle after another.

Once Henry died in 1189, Eleanor got out of lockup, and her favorite son, Richard, took the throne. Leaving Eleanor in charge of England, he soon left for the Third Crusade, where Mr. Lion-hearted managed to lose 95,000 out of 100,000 troops and get captured as well. Thanks to his ghastly performance, no one cared to raise his ransom. After Richard had languished in a Vienna prison for two years, good ole mom had to step in, write hate letters to the pope, and hustle the 130,000-mark ransom herself.

Although she'd never been keen on her youngest son, Johnny (Henry's pet), Eleanor got him out of hot water, too, when he in turn became king of England. Nearly 80 when a rebellion against John flared up, she left her fireside, threw on her by-now deplorably unstylish armor, and led her own army to crush the opposition. A classy, take-no-crap, Katharine Hepburn of a woman whose passion for life never wore out, wouldn't you say? In a neat case of art imitating life, Hepburn won an Academy Award in 1968 for playing Eleanor of Aquitaine in the memorable and semi-accurate film *The Lion in Winter*.

The Low-down
Love-gal Blues

acking modern electronics, music *aficionadas* like **Eleanor of Aquitaine** (whose granddaddy was the first troubadour of note) enjoyed their music live. With her clout as queen of France and later England, Eleanor's enthusiasm propelled troubadours into the musical celebrities of her day. As it turns out, there were women among them, too, lamenting the rocky road to courtly love and throwing out pert suggestions as to where somebody could stuff their cheatin' hearts. They were called *trobaritz*—the Provençal word for female troubadours, and it took brass for these women to get out and perform. In fact, many began as wealthy patrons of male troubadours, later taking the leap into participation and/or composing. A northern Frenchwoman who called herself **Marie of France** (thought to be a stage name for a royal in-law of Eleanor's) had hit after hit as a minstrel in the English court. No three-minute airplay here; Marie's "Lais" and other romances ran hundreds of lines. During her life, Marie's musical work—which daringly called for women to take the initiative in love-making—went international, getting translated into Norse, Middle English, and High German.

Most *trobaritz* came from southern France. Songwriter-patron **Maria de Ventadorn**, for example, who married into a long line of tune-carrying bluebloods, performed at Eleanor's court as well as her own. So far, only one of her songs has been found; in it, she advocates love relationships that even the most uppity woman of modern times could get behind: "The lady ought to do exactly for her lover/as he does for her, without regard to rank; for between two friends neither one should rule."

The **Countess of Dia** took a different tack. In one of her four

You go, girls:
12th-century trobaritz rock Europe.

surviving songs, she wrote bittersweet, modern-sounding lyrics: "With me you always act so cold, but with everyone else you're so charming." There were also female troubadours who openly expressed their earthy love for other women, such as **Beatritz de Romans,** author of an outrageous ballad to a certain Maria.

Although our biographical information on these women (at least 15 are known by name) is in tatters, fortune has left at least some of their music and lyrics, whose melodic charms can be heard electronically—and on occasion, live—just as Queen Eleanor would have liked it.

A Crusade of
Her Own

ed by France's inept King Louie IX, crusader armies headed for Egypt in 1249 to see what the pickings were, infidel-wise. On the other side, things looked grim in the Egyptian commander-in-chief's tent— the sultan had just expired. As luck would have it, the sultan's wife (or concubine, depending on whose account you believe) happened to be bivouacking with her man. Although her poetic name, **Shajar al Durr,** or Spray of Pearls, would seem to indicate otherwise, Shajar was made of tough stuff.

She kept mum about the sultan's demise, issuing bulletins each day about his "continuing recovery" to the troops and firing off new orders "signed" by the commander-in-chief. Her major challenge was the unrefrigerated corpse, of course, but this ingenious Egyptian rose to the occasion and held the situation (if not the decomposing cadaver) together.

Under her hidden leadership, the Egyptian troops bravely faced the crusader armies and soon cut off their supply routes. Plagued with both dysentery and starvation, Louie's troops beat an ignominious retreat. (With this palate of pungent battlefield aromas, small wonder nobody noticed one paltry rotting body— for whom Shajar hastily held a funeral with appropriate honors, once the crusaders were up the road.)

In 1250, the sultan's son and heir, Turan, showed up, ready to be named the next number-one despot. He was promptly killed by the pro–Spray of Pearls faction. Over the next seven years, Shajar stayed on top—but just barely. She got a lot of static, particularly from foreign leaders. Syria's top dog thought women had no place in government. Baghdad's top man was miffed, because he'd originally sent Spray of Pearls as a "from my harem to your harem" gift to the late sultan, and it just didn't seem right for the gift to do more than look decorative.

To quiet the clamor, the exasperated Sultana Shajar finally married a high military official so he could become sultan. By 1257, she'd had it with married life. She liquidated her new husband, an action that unhappily provoked a parallel reaction. Spray of Pearls was forced to jump off the citadel of Cairo into a ditch without benefit of parachute—a low end for a high-flying woman of power.

Farsighted Saint

Ever hear about television's own patron saint— **Clare of Assisi**? (Why the TV industry deserves holy protection, much less a saint, is unknown.) Like her childhood friend Francis, Clare was a rich kid, born (even before the advent of *radio*) in 1194. As a youngster, Clare admired Francis, whose way with animals and humans seemed saintly. In a world of pious frauds and holier-than-thou popes, Francis talked the talk and walked the walk; at 18, Clare followed suit, had her head shaved, and got busy begging for grits in her sackcloth. After founding the Poor Clares, an order whose actual poverty was a radical departure for nunneries of the day, Clare also helped establish the Franciscan Third Order, non-convent-based religious service open to women and men as civilians rather than nuns or monks. Before her death at 60, she clairvoyantly "saw" a Christmas Mass across town—and that is how this down-to-earth saint came to be the icon for the most unreal medium of expression.

Here. You'll need the remote.

Doctors Without Licenses— or Fees

A single physician from a ritzy family in Florence, **Jacobina Felicie** ended up in Paris. The social climate, perhaps? Don't think so—Paris of the 1300s was definitely down on dames as doctors. University-trained docs wanted to keep a lock on the profession and its rewards; beginning in 1220, French law allowed only members of the faculty of medicine to practice and needless to say, refused to admit women.

Although Mademoiselle Felicie had studied with a master doctor, she got charged with practicing *sans* degree. The penalty was a fine—and excommunication (a deterrent that deterred less and less, as more non-university-trained healers, male and female, came on the scene). This scenario was repeated several times until 1322, when she went to court to appeal her original condemnation. Gritting her teeth, Dr. Felicie brought eight witnesses—all of whom said that their doctor had refused to take any payment unless or until they got well. That gambit must have horrified the medical establishment.

Felicie also argued that Paris law went against the public good: Women doctors were especially necessary for female patients whose ailments (or modesty, or both) were such that they would not go to a male and would therefore, in all probability, die.

You will not be flabbergasted to learn that neither testimonials nor eloquence carried the day. Jacobina, two well-known female surgeons, and several male physicians (all non-U) were again excommunicated and fined. Legally, Dr. Felicie may have gone down in defeat, but it's doubtful she quit. Unlicensed medicine, practiced by determined and dedicated women and men, continued in Paris and elsewhere.

White-collar Piracy

uddenly short one husband around 1300, surprised widow **Margery Russell** gamely stepped up to the plate as head of her late lamented's import-export business in Coventry, England. Things were going pretty well until one of her ships, laden with goods worth more than 800 English pounds, got attacked en route. It had to be Spanish pirates—the infamous downside of doing business in that time and place. Margery marched into court, demanding letters of marque against Santander, Spain, the pirates' port of origin. (Letters of marque were documents from the English king that licensed a victim of high-seas robbery to seize Spanish-owned cargo—that is, goods belonging to any Spaniard, not necessarily the guilty parties—from English ports as compensation.) After Mrs. Russell got her letters, she tagged and took two Spanish ships, whose nicely bulging holds turned out to represent substantially more than the value of what the pirates stole.

This tactic, standard operating procedure among merchants of her time, provoked a roar of legal anguish from the Spaniards—ample proof that even with a late-inning start, this game dame knew how to play business hardball.

Prioress Has Happy Feet

overs of Chaucer's *Canterbury Tales* may think that the characters in his 14th-century classic are fiction, and some may be. But the prioress is based on **Madam Eglentyne**, the flesh-and-blood female head of an English nunnery. (Voluminous church records about her life and antics still exist.)

Like countless other medieval children, Eglentyne had no say-so about her entrance into the religious life. After paying a stiff dowry fee, her dad plunked his little girl into a nunnery, where she grew up learning to sing, read, speak French, and sew.

Turns out that gray-eyed Eglentyne had what it took to become prioress or head of the convent: a sweet disposition, upper-class connections, and nice table manners. At least that's what counted with the nuns who voted her in when the old prioress died. The nunnery was a business and farm as well as a religious institution, so Eglentyne as its head was supposed to keep the books straight and the convent in the black. She wasn't awfully good at it. Luckily, the bishop worked around her math phobia.

Where Eglentyne ran into religious hot water were the items known as the nun's downfall: dress, dogs, and those demonic pilgrimages. Nuns had a dress code—cover it up and make it black. Eglentyne, however, didn't see what harm could come from a few gold rings and hairpins, a silver girdle, a two-foot-tall hennin headdress, and some furs (okay, and maybe a lowcut dress with a train for special occasions). Even more distressing, she wore her veil hitched up, letting the world get a gander at her totally nude forehead. (High bare brows were a fashion must in her day—except with nuns, who were expected to cover their brows with a wimple.)

Pets in the convent were also forbidden: "Bad for discipline," the bishops said. Eglentyne, it must be admitted, had a pooch or two. But she could point to another prioress who kept a pack of dogs *and* a monkey in her room.

But the most outrageous thing Prioress Eglentyne did (and that nuns continued to do, and that bishops continued to forbid, for six centuries) was "wandering in the world." That elastic phrase meant anything from short shopping trips to town to gallivanting about the English countryside in Canterbury-style pilgrimages. Eglentyne, who traveled with another nun and three priests, chalked up more "business travel" mileage than half the bishops. (Of course, travel for male church officials was totally acceptable.)

Since A.D. 791, the clergy had been thundering at religious women to stay put. Bishops tried to get Eglentyne and the rest of them to obey this injunction for centuries. It wasn't until 1545 that every nunnery in England was dissolved by King Henry VIII—at which point all English nuns got turned out to wander in the secular world, like it or not.

So, make the doorways bigger!

An Irish Witch Hunt

ou know the Irish—they've never behaved the way they should, that is, the way the English thought they should. The tale of **Alice Kyteler** and **Petronilla of Meath** is a good example.

In the early 1300s, the pope sent an English bishop named Richard Ledrede to Kilkenny. His job was to set up an inqui-sition, nose around for witches in Ireland, and bring down a woman of standing in the com-munity. Not only would this put the fear of the papacy into the Irish ruling classes—it would put those free-spirited Celtic females in their place.

In 1324, the bishop ran across a person with the per-fect victim profile—a wealthy, three-time widow named Dame Alice Kyteler whose fourth husband had gone insane. Even better, some of

Drat! I'm one peacock short for a witchcraft indictment.

her children had been heard to whine that they didn't get what they deserved in the various wills left by this string of decedents. Bishop Ledrede, aided by an inquisition staff well trained in the arts of threats and torture, took those aggrieved kids into custody. Soon he had them composing a whole list of imagi-nary crimes: Yes, their mother had "without a doubt" killed her husbands; "everyone knew" she'd made a demonic sacrifice of nine roosters and nine peacocks; and "most probably" she was sleeping with a devil named Robin MacArt.

However, Bishop Ledrede barked up the wrong broomstick when he took on Alice. She didn't just dispute the politically motivated charges—she *took* charge. Through her various well-connected family members, she got the bishop arrested and thrown in jail for 17 days! Wisely, she left Kilkenny at that point and went to live in Dublin. Once he'd gotten sprung, the hornet-mad bishop made his case in front of Catholic officials in Dublin. This round he won, and Alice fled Ireland for England.

Due to her hasty departure, Mrs. Kyteler had to leave behind her properties and much of her wealth. The vengeful persecutors fell on those left behind—the innocent members of her family and her household. Several of her relatives ended up in prison. The hammer fell hardest on the humble people—in this case, Dame Alice's servants. (Witch hunts often did focus on the most powerless in a community—especially widows or single women without family.) They were whipped through town, excommunicated, or banished.

But Petronilla of Meath, Alice's personal servant, bore the brunt. Flogged six times and ritually tortured, she eventually confessed to being a witch. On November 3, 1324, Petronilla had the mournful distinction of being the first person in Ireland to be burnt at the stake for the heresy of sorcery.

Although Ireland would have very few other witch hunts, the trial of Kyteler and the execution of Petronilla did attract attention throughout Europe, setting precedents (from demonic sex charges to the severity of punishments) for much of what followed.

Eventually Bishop Ledrede was accused of heresy himself—twice. (Nice bit of karma, that.) It's not known if Dame Alice ever got to return to the olde sod. Her home, the oldest in Kilkenny and now known as Kyteler's Inn, still stands, a 700-year-old monument to female defiance.

Bloodshed?
Bring It On

enaissance women were famous for cutting remarks and glances. **Alessandra Giliani** of Bologna, Italy, gained fame for just plain cutting. Truth be told, it was pretty fancy knifework. A teenage prodigy who had wangled an education at the University of Bologna, she studied dissection at the side of the most famous slice-and-dice man in Italy, Mondino de Luzzi. Before long, she had become a prosector, the person who prepared dissections for anatomical studies.

In Alessandra's day, the early 1300s, anatomy researchers weren't all that clear which blood vessels were veins and which were arteries. This, of course, became horrifyingly important when someone encountered a spurting arterial wound, for example.

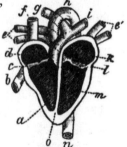

Adroit Alessandra is credited with inventing a technique for tracing the different blood vessels in the body. She drained blood from a cadaver and refilled its veins and arteries with different colored dyes that hardened, allowing even the smallest blood vessels to be seen with ease.

Teen scalpel-wielder went where few 14th-century gals cared to go.

Only 19 when her life was cut short by a tragic fire that may have also killed her mentor, she left a sorrowing fiancé named Otto Angenius. Another of Dottore de Luzzi's assistants, Angenius may have been the one who placed plaques honoring Giliani's contribution to medical science in several churches in Italy.

Dunning That Blasted King—Again

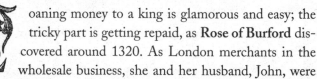

oaning money to a king is glamorous and easy; the tricky part is getting repaid, as **Rose of Burford** discovered around 1320. As London merchants in the wholesale business, she and her husband, John, were among a handful of exporters given the exclusive right to trade in a staple commodity: wool. When it came to selling English wool to the French, Rose had business acumen. The same could not be said of her spouse, who preferred his moonlighting gig as sheriff of London. Furthermore, John carried a policy of currying royal favor too far by fronting King Edward II a substantial sum to tide him over in his war against the Scottish.

Not long afterward, John died unexpectedly, and the new widow found to her dismay that King Eddie hadn't paid back any of the loan yet. Did she shrug and write off the king in the bad debts column? Quite the contrary: As executor of John's will, Rose felt obliged to go after the assets of the estate—even if it meant ticking off the royals.

With heavy heart, she petitioned the king at least five times, but England's Big Cheese was nonresponsive. Our dauntless wool widow then provided the king with a solution of her own devising. Since Rose was required to pay taxes to the crown on her own wool for export, she suggested running a tab of her duties payable and debiting them against the king's loan. This lucid proposal was an immediate hit with the uncreditworthy monarch.

Rose got repaid, and a good thing, too. A few years later, she got into debt herself, and her own goods were confiscated in the port of Dover to repay the debt. Strangely enough, no one—from King Edward on down—came to her rescue with advice, cash, or credit.

Religion from Mellow to Maniacal

Most of the folks **Margery Kempe** ran across would rather be horsewhipped than spend much time in her presence, what with her religious exhortations, haranguings for higher levels of purity, and floods of tears, to say nothing of her fainting fits, shrieks, and roars. Restful, Margery was not. Nevertheless, this middle-class English mayor's daughter who never learned to read or write led an extraordinary life.

As a teen, Margery committed a sin that doomed her to an infinity in hell. Or so she thought. After marriage and the birth of her first child, she tried to confess and failed; belief in her damned state led to a mental breakdown, followed by a direct-from-God religious experience in which she was forgiven. Margery bounced back, buying fashionable clothes again, lustily enjoying her husband, John, and having 13 more kids.

The new wardrobe and more mouths to feed added up. Margery started a brewery to increase cash flow, but it failed, as did her miller enterprise. John eventually gave up working altogether.

At length Mrs. Kempe got the notion to become a roving proselytizer for the Lord, her own religious channel, as it were. Her evangelist career was part of the Beguine movement, a non-convent-based religious way of

Lord, help me ditch Margery!

life that swept across Europe. Margery, however, aspired to be a freelance holy woman. To avoid the highly inflammable label of heretic, she needed references—so she buttonholed **Julian of Norwich,** England's top anchoress or religious recluse. A cheerful mystic who'd written *Revelations of Divine Love* from her tiny cell, Julian believed in a loving God and a simple life praising him. Nothing, however, could have prepared the 70-year-old sage for garrulous Marge, who babbled until she squeezed a testimonial out of Julian.

By this time, Kempe was having misgivings about sex and talked her husband into a legal separation—to allow them both to achieve spiritual bliss.

That done, she embarked on her greatest adventure: a pilgrimage to the Holy Land. During the first months of the journey, Kempe enraged her fellow pilgrims so much with her hysterics and preaching that they returned the money she'd paid to be part of the group and ran off. The unsinkable Kempe managed to get over the Alps with an old man as a guide and bandit-foiler. In Venice, the group ended up in the same Palestine-bound boat with Margery; she and her sorely tried companions landed in Palestine in 1414.

Christian pilgrims to Jerusalem had a tendency to sing, sob, kiss the holy places, and otherwise emote—but nobody topped Mrs. K.'s performance at the Church of the Holy Sepulchre. Moving from altar to altar, she went into convulsions, emitted extraordinary screams, and had vivid visions of Christ bleeding, which she described to the awed, half-deafened crowd.

Her place secure in paradise, Mrs. Kempe made an eventful return to England, followed by other pilgrimages to Spain and Norway. In her 60s, she hired a scribe to pen her memoirs, in which Kempe referred to herself as "this creatur." Unlucky in her hiring policies, she found the ghostwriter's mangled English and German unintelligible, and required two more scribes to finish the book. That editorial nightmare, however, was nothing compared to the time it took to get the book in print. A mere 503 years after her hotly emotional words were put to paper, *The Book of Margery Kempe* came off the press—giving us a look at a world by turns religious, raucous, and ripely real.

The Real Deal and the Faux Joans of Arc

ew teens in history have gotten the attention that Joan of Arc has. Fewer still have gotten it by being gutsy as well as good. At age 13, Joan heard heavenly voices telling her to help the weak French monarch Charles VII defend his kingship against the English and liberate the besieged French city of Orléans. Within three years, she'd lobbied the powerful women around the king, gotten Charles to give her an army, and was leading 4,000 enthusiastic troops in a suit of dazzling silver armor.

On April 28, 1429, Joan freed Orléans; by summer, the English invaders were history, and Charles was officially crowned at Reims. When the new king asked Joan to name her reward, this altruistic miss said, "How about lowering the taxes for Domrémy [her home town] and Greux?" The surprised monarch complied.

But war generals (even volunteer ones) are like showbiz folks—only as good as their last triumph. After Joan failed to take Paris, the English nabbed her, and the French did nothing. At her heresy/witchcraft trial, her accusers cited such "occult" behavior as the wearing of men's clothing. On May 30, 1431, the maid of Orléans, 19 and still a virgin (although her English captors did their best to change her status while they had her imprisoned), was burned at the stake. Joan of Arc died with

amazing stoicism. Her secret weapon? Belief in God and the role she was destined to play in her country's deliverance. A mere 500 years later, the gallant teen was declared a saint.

The unflinching example of this heroic martyr attracted a surprising number of suicidally devoted female wannabes (or wanna-cash-ins). Among them was **Jeanne La Férone**, who asserted she could cure ulcers as well as lead armies. When her other boast of being a virgin also proved incorrect, La Férone was sentenced to tour downtown Le Mans in a dunce cap.

Another copycat was **Jehane, Maid of Sermaize**, who bummed around in men's clothing, preaching and hitting on folks for meals and lodging. A third voice-guided contender named **Pierronne** was said to have fought in the French army; like her heroine, Mademoiselle P. was condemned to be burned at the stake.

The tales about **Claude-Jeanne des Armoises**, most prominent (and written-about) of the Joan imitators, were legion. One version asserts that she fought in the pope's army with such distinction she was given command of troops. This Jeanne also bore two children and thus was reprimanded for a missing hymen, to which she replied: "My value is not dependent on virginity."

According to another version of her story, Claude-Jeanne appeared in the city of Metz five years after Joan of Arc's death and soon convinced two of Joan's brothers that she'd escaped the bonfire. Later she married Robert des Armoises, who also bought her story. In 1437, she visited Orléans and got a "thanks for saving us from the siege" cash bonanza from credulous citizens. Despite her obvious impersonation skills, Claude-Jeanne ended up in irons and had to declare herself an official Joan of Arc imposter in 1440. She may have escaped a high-Fahrenheit fate, however. An inquisitor regretfully mentions "the one who got away," referring to a Joan reincarnation who escaped being burned alive. In a brutal era, that was a major accomplishment.

Battling armies, inquisitors, and tax collectors.

Molto Talento

"Renaissance woman" doesn't offer enough scope to describe **Onorata Rodiana,** a versatile native of Castelleone, Italy, whose talent for art was surpassed only by a bigger one for banditry. A fresco-painting *maestra*, Onorata was hired by the Marquis Gabrino Fondolo to decorate his palace in Cremona. While she was working on her painting commission, a lecher around the palace tried to *fondolo* our Onorata. She dropped her brushes, picked up a weapon (her palette knife?), stabbed the would-be rapist, and left the vicinity in a big hurry, disguised as a man.

The marquis—a tyrant who would come to a bad end in 1425—pitched a fit, sending his troops after her but with zero results. After he cooled down, he put the word out on the street that Onorata could return any time, stabbing incident forgotten. Well, the marquis might find it easy to overlook the attack on Rodiana's person, but she was not about to buy into his forgive-and-forget approach.

Anyway, she'd already found a new métier; by now, this marvelously flexible miss had plunged enthusiastically into a career field that offered more scope for her newfound skills. Rodiana joined a band of *condottieri*, the mercenaries for hire who made life in Renaissance Italy so exciting.

Never good at following orders, Onorata was soon giving them, as she climbed the corporate criminal ladder to head up her own band. Over the next 30 years, the many-faceted Rodiana found she could have it all: One week she was cross-dressing and masterminding the next plunder and pillage campaign; the next week, she would take on the occasional fresco job.

Although her art career had its peaks and valleys, banditry certainly didn't. Like modern attorneys, mercenaries throughout Italy knew the way to success in business was to keep on billing. Rodiana and her pay-per-pillage professionals got really good at milking would-be rulers, switching sides to milk those clients' sworn enemies, prolonging small wars, and keeping regional hatreds alive—all done from horseback to minimize casualties. (*Condottieri* had their own code of ethics regarding bloodshed and major injuries, which resembled that of contemporary professional wrestling.)

The only thing our Renaissance rover forgot was: You can't go home again. In 1472, she returned to Castelleone, which was busy being besieged by the Venetians. Always a softie for her hometown, Onorata tried to ride to the rescue, and was killed—nonstop action to the last frame.

PART THREE

UPPITY WOMEN
OF
Renaissance Times

1450 – 1750

❖ ❖ ❖ ❖ ❖

CHRISTOPHER·COLVMBVS

*Christopher Columbus, one-night
stand expert of the 15th century.*

Old-world Leave-behinds

he personal life of Christopher Columbus, perhaps the most written-about man in history, remains *terra incognita*. What we know about the loves of his life is substantially less than Columbus knew about the location of India—and the scraps we do have about Felipa and the two Beatrices show a side to the admiral that wouldn't win any sensitive-male awards.

A lanky vagabond from a humble Italian family who'd made his way to Portugal, he got in the habit of going to mass at a certain convent in order to meet **Felipa Perestrello**, the daughter of one of Lisbon's tonier families. The two hit it off and married; after the wedding, they moved to the islands of Madeira and Porto Santo, where son Diego was born about 1480. Felipa barely lived to 30. After her death, Chris moved to Spain, then dumped his son with the monks at La Rábida monastery while he lobbied Queen Isabella and King Ferdinand for financing. Busy with Moor-expelling, the royals told him, "We'll get back to you," and put him on hold for years.

During that time, Columbus hung out in Córdoba, making friends with Jimmy Haraña—and even tighter friends with Jim's cousin **Beatriz de Haraña**, a good-looking orphan of 20. In August 1488, Bea gave birth to a boy she named Fernando. "Wham, bam, *gracias*, ma'am," Chris had left the building— possibly the province—by then.

When Queen Isabella finally gave Columbus's expedition a go-ahead, Chris cruised by Córdoba to give a quick hello to his son, then went south to order the monks to drop his older son, Diego, at Bea's house (once he was safely at sea, you get the feeling).

In 1493, the triumphant mariner returned from his epic voyage to a major fiesta across Spain. Columbus swung by Córdoba, said, "I'm back! Thanks for babysitting—oh, and *adiós*

forever," to Beatriz, and picked up his 5- and 13-year-old sons.
Supposedly to protect his interests while he was at sea, Chris got
his sons appointed as court pages to Queen Isabella. The plot
thickens. The hard-hearted social climber had fallen for a second Beatrix during his first voyage. While taking on supplies in
the Canary Islands, he met a luscious widow from Gomera
whose social connections and physical attributes were equally
impeccable. Their whirlwind romance lasted *four whole days*. A
year later, the love-crazed explorer stopped by Gomera, where
Beatrix Peraza y Bobadilla welcomed his fleet with fireworks,
cannons, and most likely, a wed-and-stay-put ultimatum. Not
being *that* crazed, Chris took a pass; Bea, however, took some
heat when a local gossiped that she and C.C. had split a ham-
mock. Bea coolly invited the gossiper to tea; for dessert, she had
her servants string him from her rafters, later adorning his own
house with the corpse. Her reputation for virtue (and ferocity)
restored, she went on to marry a home-based noble.

His Canary Island fling notwithstanding, Chris finally had a
wee twinge of conscience about Bea the first, archival documents
show. In 1493, the palimony-allergic admiral gave her the rent
concession for some butcher shops in Córdoba—a perk that
brought in 10,000 *maravedis* a year. (Sound like meaty money? It
wasn't.) In 1502, Chris ordered son Diego to award Bea a similar
pension. Meanwhile, sons and father became wealthy and honored; Bea Haraña got into debt, struggled to live on her pensions,
and died alone—without so much as a visit from either her son or
the man who might have been her only significant other.

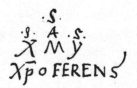

Outwitting an Impaler Husband

From 1462 on, **Ilona Szilágyi** kept finding marriage proposals with a Transylvania postmark in her mailbox. First cousin of Hungarian king Matthias, Ilona belonged to the snooty Corvinus clan. The mystifying proposals were from sadist and social climber Vlad "my fiends call me Dracula" the Impaler, the prince of three measly provinces. Ilona was contemptuous; why, the man didn't even terrorize a real country! However, politics—or cousinly payback—intervened, and in 1467, King Matthias gave the green light for Ilona to wed the dread Vlad.

Dracula had to jump a few hoops to win his woman, being locked up in a castle, more political refugee than prince, at the time of the nuptials. Matthias made him promise to annihilate the invading Turks and convert to Catholicism. Vlad did not have to give up his favorite leisure activities, however, such as nailing diplomats' hats to their heads.

As a wedding gift, Matthias gave the couple a house in Pest, "right across the river from Buda—you can't miss it." Ilona settled in to procreate as Mrs. Dracula, and before long, several baby Dracs graced the premises.

In late 1476, Ilona had a tremendous stroke of luck: Mr. Impaler died in battle at age 45 and soon had his own head displayed on a stake in Constantinople. Ilona moved back to Buda to enjoy her favorite leisure activity— succession intrigues. Eventually

Some prince—he doesn't even terrorize a whole country.

she saw her son on the Wallachian throne for a nanosecond, before the real bloodshed began among Drac descendants and would-be Vlads.

Female Nostradamus

ften called "Mother," **Ursula Shipton** operated during the reign of King Henry VIII. Born about 1488 in a small cave in Yorkshire, she became one of London's most colorful characters, with a rep far and wide as a witch, a prophetess, and a seer or scryer. Need a look into the future? A love charm? A hate bracelet? Mother Shipton was your merchant of magick.

In Renaissance times, being identified as a witch was normally the best way to shorten your life span. Not so with Mother Shipton. She lived well into her 70s, a clairvoyant figure around whom popular legend swirled. And no wonder: Even if her extrasensory powers were all showwomanship, she was a weird-looking individual. Ursula had an unusually long head, fiery eyes, and a crooked nose, covered with what were described by awed contemporaries (including her husband) as "multi-colored phosphorescent warts."

The female Nostradamus of her day, Ursula Shipton aroused great excitement with her predictions regarding the fate of famous men and the end of the world (in her view, 1999 looked dreadful). Although she was probably illiterate, her fame endured for centuries, and accounts (mostly bogus) of her utterances continue to be published into the 21st—check your supermarket's trashy book rack.

Renaissance Friends with Benefits

ame artists in Renaissance Italy got gushed over plenty. On occasion, however, the tables were turned. Michelangelo, for instance, couldn't say enough good things—verbally and artistically—about his best friend, **Vittoria Colonna**, the marchioness of Pescara. (Truly "just good friends," these two really had a platonic relationship. He was 64, and she was 49—which helped.)

A Roman noblewoman of taste and discernment, Vittoria centered her life around poetry, the arts, and religious questions. Married at 19, she was soon separated from her husband by war, but they wrote reams of letters to each other. The letters survived, he did not—prompting the marchioness to mope a spell at an island retreat, writing religious verse. Eventually Colonna embraced life again, becoming a major player in Rome's intellectual life, an authority on Plato, and a published poet at age 48.

With sinking heart, Vittoria saw another sonnet in Mikey's hand.

What she didn't embrace was another husband. Vittoria became a secular nun (the habit-optional way to go), living in the convent of San Silvestro. From about 1536 on, she and Michelangelo—whose studio was close by—became tighter than ticks. Vittoria inspired Mike to write dozens of sonnets and other poems (which, upon sampling, inspire most readers to be thankful that he wisely concentrated on painting and sculpture!).

More than a poetic muse, however, Vittoria was a spiritual rock, his teacher, his intellectual sparring partner, and the sole person in whom he confided his perplexity and anguish about the rapidly changing world they both lived in, and how to survive in it. Vittoria's simple and fervent beliefs influenced Michelangelo far more than the emotional fireworks of the Counter-Reformation, the Catholic Church's attempt at cleaning its own house. In gratitude, he painted three great works for her—today, however, only copies remain of her *Pietà*, *Crucifixion*, and *Christ with the Woman of Samaria*.

The sole thing Michelangelo regretted about his relationship with Vittoria Colonna was their good-bye. On February 20, 1547, the woman whose spirit he had communed with for so long died. As he later told a friend, he greatly wished he'd kissed her face, instead of merely her hand, in farewell.

When Tolerance in Spain Was Mainly on the Wane

he young woman who would become **Queen Isabella I** of Castile ate ambition for breakfast. As a teen who'd already survived family intrigues, she was adept at military strategy and negotiation. When she married her mild-mannered second cousin Ferdinand in 1469, Isabella insisted on parity. She would run the kingdom of Castile, Ferdie would run Aragon, and as a team they would rule Spain. Besides being full of political acumen, Isabella was an amazing horsewoman on the battlefield—which may account for the miscarriages she suffered, including one during the siege of Toledo in 1475. Nevertheless, she did her queen-as-breeder duty, birthing five kids in 15 years.

As a youngster, Isabella hadn't gotten a polished education. As queen, she remedied that by hiring the most celebrated female intellectuals of the day to teach Latin and other subjects to her and her children. Both these women were more than tutors. Educated in Italy, writer and Latin scholar **Beatrix Galindo** also had a medical degree and taught at the University of Salamanca. In later life, she founded the Hospital of the Holy Cross that stands in the Madrid neighborhood still called La Latina in Bea's honor. The older of the two, **Francisca de Lebrija**, daughter of humanist scholar and writer Antonio de Lebrija, taught at the University of Alcalá outside Madrid and was famous for her rhetoric lectures.

This golden coin is called an "excellente," which seems an ironic comment on Isabella's reign.

As their pupil and as queen, Isabella was bright, energetic, pious, and visionary. She lacked only one key quality: religious tolerance. Rigid Catholics, she and Ferdinand began a costly ten-year war, their goal being to eject, convert, or exterminate all Moors, Gypsies, and Jews. They also put the Spanish Inquisition and its thugs into motion, creating a new wave of witch hunts and heresy trials.

When the Moors surrendered, all parties signed the Treaty of Granada, which gave some protections to Moorish and Jewish citizens. In January 1492, when the treaty was to take effect, Isabella and the king changed their minds, swayed by arguments—"You're selling out Christianity!"—from the infamous inquisitor Torquemada. In the treaty's place they issued the heinous Alhambra Decree, which ordered all Jews out of Spain by July 31 of that year on pain of death. (That decree was not officially revoked until 1968, by the Second Vatican Council.)

This tragic turnabout has often been overshadowed by the glitzier events of 1492, namely Isabella's underwriting of Christopher Columbus. He'd hung out at the court for eons, wheedling for funds to find a shortcut to "the Indies." The queen and Chris had much in common; both were tall, blue-eyed, and had grandiose regard for their God-ordained roles. King Ferdinand let Isabella spend her own money on this cross-ing-the-ocean notion. Since she'd already hocked her best jewels to get the Moors out, Columbus got the cheapest ships going.

Although Columbus's initial voyage didn't bring back much in the way of swag, the feat was showy. The New World took on a golden aura, and Isabella's role in its discovery by Europeans was touted on coins, such as the *excellente*, on which the queen and king were pictured. With the benefit of historical hindsight, we can see now that Columbus's exploration unleashed another cruel human rights disaster, this time in the New World. If only Isabella had been more willing to live and let live, as the Moorish rulers before her had treated their subjects for seven centuries, how much more excellent and golden her reign would gleam today.

Luther's Stoutest Rib

P rotestant rebel Martin Luther was in a quandary. His manifesto contained the radical idea that clergy should marry, and monks and nuns everywhere were saying, "Right on!" In 1523, the issue got personal. At Germany's Nimbschen convent, 12 nuns wanted to leave their cloister and asked for help. Sneaking even the slimmest nun out of a nunnery was tricky—UPS didn't pick up in the area.

But Martin pulled it off, orchestrating a Great Escape in

herring barrels on a delivery wagon. He then found mates for everyone but **Katie von Bora**. Twenty-six-year-old Bora had brains and chutzpah; she leaned on Luther to find her a suitable spouse. "Someone like . . . oh, you, for instance," she hinted.

Luther was thunderstruck. "I'm not good husband material—gosh, I'll probably be burned at the stake in a year or two."

She persisted, though, and in 1525, the unromantic 42-year-old and Katie held a BYOBB (bring your own beer barrel) wedding party. Their marriage was a mutual admiration partnership, despite Martin's lack of earning power and poor personal habits. (Before Katie, he'd let a year go by without washing his bed sheets.) He called her "my lord Katie" and "my rib." Although Luther's earnings were slim, wealthy supporters gave them a recycled cloister as a home, and sent wine, food, and clothes at intervals.

The woman who housebroke Martin Luther.

Enterprising Katie developed her own orchard, garden, and fish pond, while doing the slaughtering, planting the fields, reading a Bible verse or two, and birthing six Luthers. She also made and sold great beer. At their home, she took in 40 paying boarders and dozens of shirt-tale relatives. Katie loved the give-and-take at her dinner table, crowded with freeloading Protestant celebrities, religious refugees, and friends.

Although Martin Luther warned, "No good ever came out of female domination," he also learned about the sacred "honey-do" contract between a man and wife. As he wrote, "Get you a wife and then your mind, however fussy, will become straight as a ribbon. It will be reduced to one idea: Do and think as she wishes."

In the end, this oh-so-pragmatic marriage became a love

match. As Martin said, "Katie, you have a husband that loves you. Let someone else be empress."

After Luther's death in 1546, Katie continued coping. Twice she and family had to flee invading armies, then rebuild. Then she suffered a driving accident and was thrown into a ditch. After months of illness, she died, saying, "I will stick to Christ as a burr to a topcoat."

"Unyoked Is Best!"

sister in a religious order in Holland, **Anna Bijns** ran her own school and taught during the mid-1500s. Remembered chiefly as a writer, at times Bijns shocked the bejesus out of her audiences. Through her plays and poems, she attacked Lutheranism and the

social ills she thought it brought. One of her surviving works was *Marika of Nijmeghen*, an early version of the Faust legend. In it, a female protagonist sells her soul to the devil in return for instruction in the liberal arts (in Anna's day a strange assortment of rhetoric, music, logic, grammar, geometry, arithmetic, and alchemy). You might call the dialogue wooden—especially the devil's lines, which invariably begin, "Well, my pretty, you can trust me." Feminist Anna had

A Faust-talking woman is the devil's work.

fresh things to say about female independence, however. She advocated taking a pass on marriage, "even if he's rich and noble,"

calling the single gal a "lord and mistress, none ever lived better."
One of her poems was called "Unyoked Is Best! Happy the
Woman Without a Man." Did her words inflame? I'd say so: For
publishing Bijns's first collection of writings, her printer actually
got executed!

Ink on Paper Pioneers

B etween 1500 and 1600, *la belle* France was especially *belle* for women who loved putting ink on
paper. Paris was a high-tech hotbed of printing and
publishing where at least 54 literate
ladies made their mark in print, as a listing of
Parisian printers along with legal contracts
signed by women show.

One standout was **Yolande Bonhomme**,
a shrewd printer who profited by
publishing more than 200 titles,
most of them religious tomes. Like
other publishers, she sold her books
in other parts of Europe. Yolande had a
nimble marketing sense; when sales of
her illustrated books of hours sagged,
she shifted gears to regional titles and
scholarly works.

French women of the time were
able to enter this field because of fair
laws regarding property and inheritance; the family-run nature of
printing; and expectations of female
competency. Husband-wife and
father-daughter collaborations were

Stop the presses!
Romance is hot again!

common. Even more common were wives who became widows and took over the business.

One such bereaved widow, **Madame Trepperel**, cranked out 121 romance novels, some under her own imprint, others with her son-in-law—until he likewise died. Up stepped her daughter, **Macee**, who handled the presses with her son, Denis. In 1545, after Macee and son expired, **Jehanne de Marnef**, a third-generation family member, took over.

Well-educated **Charlotte Guillard** became the nonpareil of literacy in her day. A much-married, triple-widowed business-woman, she first wed Berthold Rembolt, co-owner of the prestigious Soleil d'Or publishing house. The couple eventually built a hotel that housed their family and their entire workforce. Typically, it took three to five men to run one press; most print shops had five presses. Throw in bookbinders, typecasters, bean-counters, and cooks (it being customary to feed the help), and Charlotte had a factory-sized payroll. After Rembolt died and widow Charlotte became CEO, she employed her niece **Marye Baugaurd**; pay records still exist for Marye's work as editor.

In her later marriages, Charlotte also inherited a bookstore. Publishing continuously for 50 years, this paragon produced hun-dreds of titles, from civil law books, dictionaries, and scientific works to classics in Latin and Greek, winning acclaim for her business savvy—and for her insistence on the quality of content and materials. Despite the feast or famine nature of publishing, Guillard provided generous marriage dowries for her many nieces (including Marye Baugaurd) and for numerous poor women without such means.

In contrast to the lively printing-publishing scene enjoyed by women in France, women had a tougher time in places like England and Denmark. Nevertheless, records show that at least 17 women worked in London as printers and booksellers. There were smaller numbers in Denmark, where guild regulations stipulated that a female printer-publisher could work solo only for three years before remarrying into the guild, or liquidating her business.

Tart Tongue but Kept Her Head

Sometimes 'twas a far far better thing to have loved and lost a throne—especially if the throne in question was occupied by the hefty haunches of one Henry VIII of England. That's what **Christina of Denmark** thought, anyway. In 1538, Henry was spouse-hunting again, having lost wife number three to childbed fever. His globe-trotting artist, Hans Holbein, painted Christina's likeness—and the king loved it. As a bonus, this dimpled duchess, Danish by birth and already a duke's widow at 16, resembled Madge Shelton, the saucy intern at the English court who'd given Henry palpitations (or something) during the pregnancy of the late queen Anne Boleyn.

Portrait of a serial spouse-shredder.

Christina also loved hunting, card playing, and other Henry hobbies. As the icing on the Euromerger cake, she was the niece of Charles V, Holy Roman emperor. The English ambassador began negotiations, telling the duchess that by marrying Henry "you'll be matched with the most gentle Gentleman that liveth; his nature so benign and pleasant, that I think till this day no man hath heard many angry words pass his mouth." Christina knew a tall tale when she heard it. "If I had two heads, I'd be happy to offer King Henry one of them!" was her possibly apocryphal but much-repeated reply.

Head over heels for Henry? No, thanks.

Power Mom, Printer Daughter

The life story of **Gracia Mendes Nasi** reads like an international thriller, starting with her aliases: Named Hannah but called Gracia (Hannah's Spanish translation), she also answered to the Christianized name of Beatriz de Luna Miques. Why? Because in her day (circa 1510–1569), Jews—the prime scapegoats of the time—continued to endure persecution and expulsion from countries they had made their own.

Originally from Spanish Aragon, Gracia's family fled to Portugal before her birth to escape the ferocious Inquisition and expulsion campaigns of Catholic rulers Isabella and Ferdinand. In Portugal they became *conversos*, or new Christians, but the family never jettisoned Judaism. At 18, the teen wed Francisco, linking her wealthy clan with the Mendes banking-finance family, who were also crypto-Jews. The couple built a thriving international business, trading in pepper and other spices.

Gracia had just eight years to enjoy married life before becoming a widow with a daughter, Brianda Reyna, to care for. That same crummy year, the pope du jour ordered an inquisition for Portugal. Gathering up her kinfolk and that critical instrument for flight, her fortune, Gracia hopped around Europe, looking for a place to make a life and be Jewish, too. They made a pit stop in England (nope); dallied in Antwerp (money welcome, religion not very); and settled in Venice until the bubonic plague broke out and Jews were naturally thought to be the cause. It was moving time again.

When she and entourage reached Ferrara, Gracia thought she'd finally found a safe haven in Italy. For the first time, she openly used her Jewish name. By now a seasoned businesswoman, this maven of moves also became an ardent activist. Using her network of business agents, she and her brother-in-law set up a 16th-century underground railroad that enabled thousands of Jews from around Europe to escape bonfires, torture, and other dire fates. Thanks to her business moxie, her wealth, her philanthropy, and her personal convictions, Gracia was able to defy kings, popes, and high-level officials. When trade embargos, showdowns, and other defiance failed to work, she simply bribed them.

Gracia had just gotten used to Italy when trouble brewed again. This time, however, somebody offered her asylum—the sultan of Turkey, no less. In 1553, 17 years after exiting Portugal, Gracia and family settled in Constantinople, where she became the most influential woman of her day.

Meanwhile, her bright, bookish daughter, known as Reyna, married kinsman Joseph Nasi, urged on by her high-voltage mama. Joseph became the matriarch's point man, running the family's merchant fleet and developing a trade network for wines. Later **Reyna Mendes Nasi** began to feed her own passion, setting up as a printer. For years, she published books in Hebrew for the large Jewish community in Turkey.

Tiberias and the Sea of Galilee, site of Gracia's dream home.

Gracia continued to support the community, building hospitals and synagogues. As welcoming as Constantinople was, however, she became convinced that Palestine was their rightful home. With this in mind, she offered a few zillion ducats to the Ottoman Turks (who owned Palestine at the time) to set up a Jewish settlement in Tiberias on the Sea of Galilee. She consummated the deal, but it's thought that Gracia didn't live long enough to settle in the community of 60,000 on the Galilee shore.

This extraordinary woman, whose name still appears on synagogues and other buildings, was honored by the state of Israel in October 2010, in commemoration of the 500th anniversary of her birth.

The Agony and the Ecstasy of Art

 "As long as I live, I will have control over my being." That vow came from the lips of **Artemisia Gentileschi**, famous as a painter in the 17th century—and notorious as the plaintiff in a Roman rape trial as sensational as any in the 21st century.

After teaching his precocious daughter everything he knew, Artemisia's father, Orazio, looked for a more experienced mentor. The credulous man settled on Agostino Tassi, somehow failing to note his apparent prior conviction for arranging his own wife's murder!

Tassi's lessons with Artemisia were at first chaperoned by another woman, but the persuasive ruffian soon got rid of the escort long enough to hit on Artemisia. When he found seduction a hard sell to the strong-minded 18-year-old, he raped her. After Orazio learned of Artemisia's assault, he insisted that Tassi marry his daughter. Tassi laughed in his face. Orazio pressed charges, and the matter came to trial.

Although the year was 1612, trials still used methods from the Dark Ages, including torturing material witnesses to "prove" their veracity on the witness stand. The trial transcripts still exist, showing that for the five months of her testimony officials used a device that looped around Artemisia's fingers, inflicting excruciating pain. She remained adamant, telling the truth even when it hurt. Tassi was convicted, but after only eight months in jail won aquittal.

After her bruising ordeal in Rome, most gossipy of cities, Artemisia fled to Florence, where she became the first woman allowed into the painters' guild. She also had a short-lived marriage to Pietro Vincenzo. Their daughter, Palerma Vincenzo, inherited her mother's talent.

A Baroque artist of the Caravaggio school, Artemisia painted shattering scenes of human drama. She took hackneyed biblical subjects, such as Judith killing Holofernes, and turned them into autobiography. Gentileschi healed herself while getting the best sort of revenge—an artistic legacy of more than 30 extant paintings. As an adult, Artemisia lived independently. It's clear she knew her own worth. She once sent a painting to a blueblooded patron with this note: "This will show your Lordship what a woman can do."

An extraordinary artist from Cremona, Italy, **Sofonisba Anguissola**, born around 1532, was one of seven children. Her dad wrote to Michelangelo about her talent, which started a rich correspondence. She sent drawings; he challenged and critiqued her.

At 27, Sofonisba nabbed her first big commission, as court painter for King Philip II of Spain. After 20 years at the Madrid court, she fell in love with a Sicilian noble. The king footed the bill for the wedding and gave her a juicy dowry, even though the couple moved back to Italy. A few years later, her husband died of plague. Still without a court painter, King Philip asked the

*Sofonisba pointed out gender hypocrisies of her day on canvas,
and sold them to eager buyers, mostly male.*

new widow for a return engagement. While she was sailing back
to Spain, sparks flew again, this time with the ship's captain, and
she wed him.

Sofonisba's most-painted subject (like that of Rembrandt)
was her own face, rendered with candor and dignity. Her
fame traveled internationally, and clients clamored for her
self-portraits; many still exist. Lucky in love, lucky in fortune
and fame, Sofonisba took aim at the gender hypocrisies of her
day in such paintings as *The Chess Game*, featuring her
charming sisters playing the traditionally male game. One
sister holds the winning black queen—the painter's symbolic
way of saying that women's status should equal men's. This
grand, no-flies-on-me woman lived to be 93, still visited by
younger artists seeking advice.

Celestial Siblings

A determined Dane in an era when most girls played demure, **Sophia Brahe** was crazy about all things celestial. As her Latin-spouting big brother Tycho, already a celebrity astronomer, said, *"Ad astra per aspera"*—you can get to the stars, but it's a rocky road. First she had to get a scientific education. Forbidden to attend males-only school, she harassed her parents until she got home tutoring in math, music, astrology, alchemy, and classical literature. On her own, she pursued astronomy, which delighted her brother. He was already getting generous sums from the Danish government for his research work on comets and chemistry.

Uranisborg, the palatial observatory where Sophia worked and star-gazed.

By her teens, Sophia had become Tycho's assistant at Uraniborg, his observatory and scientific community on the island of Hven, where she helped with the computations for a lunar eclipse in 1573. Even sexier sky events were in store; the great comet of 1577, for instance, which blazed across the heavens when Sophia was 21.

Eventually, Sophia had to drop her astronomical workload and marry a high-born gent from Skane, a part of southern Sweden annexed to Denmark at the time. Already comfortable, Sophia became wealthy with her first marriage. Ten years later, her spouse died; she returned to her studies, tackling chemistry, biology, and horticulture. She dug deeper into homeopathic medicine and alchemy, inventing a "pest elixir" she believed would combat the plague. Sophia became a regular fixture at

Uraniborg. Tycho needed her help with fixing the positions of 1,000 stars for his magnum opus. Sophia also mingled well with the science crowd, who stayed on the island for months at a time. One wonk she took a special shine to was Erik Lange, an upper-crust alchemist. She checked their astrological charts—a perfect match! Erik owned as much real estate as Sophia, so there was fiscal equilibrium as well as zodiacal alignment. In 1590, they got engaged.

Soon this made-in-heaven merger began to crumble. Sophia's fiancé squandered his fortune on alchemy experiments, and then hightailed it to Germany to evade creditors—and look for gullible new patrons. Sophia still believed she and Erik were fated to end up together; by now, not even big brother was on her side. After Tycho's death in 1601, and over shouts of "You're disowned!" from the family, she left Denmark to marry her alchemist in 1602. At age 46, Sophia got her first dose of real poverty when they had to return Erik's clothes to the pawnshop after the wedding. By 1608, Erik was living in Prague, the marriage a bust. Having run through her fortune, Sophia returned to Denmark and to her first love, science. It had been a long and rocky road, but Sophia probably read that in the stars, too.

Ninja Head Coach

shrewd Japanese widow who worked all the angles, **Chiyome** knew it's better to be at the top of a pyramid scheme than scuffling on the ground floor. With that principle in mind, around 1560 she started her own rent-a-ninja business, training girls to become *kunoichi,* or "deadly flowers," as they were called.

Before ninjas mutated into the cartoons and avatars they are today, they worked as spies during most of Japan's thousand-year

medieval period. In this class-conscious society, samurai war-
lords used ninjas to do their dirty work: spread subversion,
discover enemy plans, or knock off unwanted political figures or
other samurais. Popular as they were as a labor force, ninjas got
about as much prestige and pay as burger-flippers in a fast-food
chain. Thinking volume business, Chiyome saw it would make
more economic sense to train ninjas rather than be one; as the
not-so-bereaved spouse of a warlord, she enjoyed a home-alone
situation that gave her the necessary privacy to set up a clan-
destine school.

Traditionally, ninjahood got passed down from one generation
to another within ninja families, most of whom lived in remote villages in the Iga and Koga districts. Our female Fagin, however, had
the clever idea of taking in the throwaway kids of her time—
orphans, runaways, and the like. How sweet, the neighbors
thought, failing to notice the whizzing sound of throwing stars.

In her school, Chiyome's trainees learned to use martial arts,
knives, swords, spears, and an ax-spear combo called the halberd.
Deadly flowers also had to improvise, turning anything into a
killing tool. Hairpins got dipped in poison. A lady's fan got
sharpened to a razor point. Her ninjas carried an array of projec-
tiles, steel claws, blinding powders, and other cool stuff, lashed to
their waists with a sash called an *obi*—a nine-foot-long piece of
cloth that could double as climbing gear and field bandage.

Most of the girls looked forward to wearing the "cloak of
darkness" black ninja garb (so slimming!); sometimes, however,
they used street clothes. Boss Chiyome often got assignments
that called for womanly wiles—for which her deadly flowers had
to drag out the kimono with the plunging neckline.

Besides weapons training, the young and the invisible spent
countless hours tree-climbing, hiding underwater, and learning
to dislocate their joints for easier escape from small places or
from being tied up. No matter how slick they got, however, there
was one situation they were highly unlikely to get out of—their
bondage to the redoubtable Madame Chiyome.

Basque Nun Turned Top Gun

ife sentence as a nun in a convent? Fate worse than death, thought Basque spitfire **Catalina de Erauso** upon reaching those troubled teenage years. Stuffed into a nunnery by her folks, Catalina ran away in March of 1600. Her goal: to join the opposite sex. Unlike other women who put on men's togs and told the barber "short all around," Catalina wasn't chasing a sweetheart, husband, or a prized client—this tall, well-muscled tomboy craved an adventurous life. And she got it. A natural at cross-dressing, swordplay, and skullduggery, Catalina freelanced across Spain; three years later, she earned (or stole) her passage to the New World. Once she started rambling across Panama, Peru, and Chile, Erauso really came into her own as a brawler, gambler, and soldier of fortune.

Occasionally she held a legitimate job. She joined the army, became a second lieutenant, and served under her unsuspecting older brother Michael, fighting the natives. But Catalina had a hair-trigger temper and a real talent with pistols, daggers, and swords. Not counting battlefield slayings, she murdered eight men, only one of whom she was sorry about—the "mistaken identity" killing of her own sibling in a nighttime duel.

For 20-odd (very odd) years, gender-bender Erauso roamed the Wild West highlands of the Peruvian Andes, in and out of jail, evading the law (and twice the hangman's noose) by a hair. Like other charismatic loners, she attracted female admirers but evaded the snare of intimacy or matrimony.

In 1620, finding herself in a worse jam than usual, Catalina sought refuge with a bishop, to whom she confessed her true story. Despite her seamy life, Erauso was still a virgin; this astounded the bishop more than anything. As people learned of her, they seemed to feel that virginity compensated for her prior sins! She returned to Spain a celebrity; a gifted talker, she schmoozed the king into awarding her a pension and a return ticket, then visited the pope, who was tickled enough to give Catalina, now widely known as the Lieutenant Nun, the all-clear to wear male clothing. When last heard of, Catalina was mule-driving in Mexico, calling herself Antonio de Erauso.

Even before her death, legends built around the Lieutenant Nun. Probably penniless when she died, this scalawag left something priceless—an autobiography of her capers. It gives glimpses of a bold and original mind—and the price she paid for her lone-gun, don't-tie-me-down life.

Shipwright by Day, Amazon by Night

A Dutch brewer's daughter in 16th-century Haarlem, **Kenau Hasselaar** didn't just say "Ya, ya" to the first set of clog shoes that came to her door. She married a hometown shipwright, who built new ships and repaired old ones while she happily built a home life, until widowed at 35 with four kids to support. Fortunately, Haarlem was a bustling port and trade center, strategically located a tulip bulb's throw from Amsterdam.

In 1562, widow Hasselaar registered with city authorities as an independent shipwright and jumped into the high-mileage life of medieval business folk. You had to be hard as cheese rind to make it as an entrepreneur. (In fact, Dutch female traders became famous in the Old World and the New as very tough cookies.)

Kenau put in long days, working the Holland-Belgium-Sweden-Denmark circuit. Besides going after new ship orders and customers, she had to contend with tax-happy officials, lawsuit-happy colleagues, integrity-challenged suppliers, a recalcitrant workforce, and slick financiers—a business world quite like today,

Spaniards take Haarlem. Kenau and defenders take it back, finally.

in fact. With her native wit and growing business acumen, Kenau soon became a person of standing even among the tough-to-impress Dutch.

Her feats as head of Hasselaar shipwright enterprises paled beside her actions as a loyal citizen. The predominantly Protestant city of Haarlem exploded in protest around 1568 at the Catholic rule being imposed by the Spanish Duke of Alba and his crowd. Hostilities broke out; along with other women, Kenau and her sister Amaron grabbed swords and jumped to the city's defense. Kenau organized a battalion of 300 female patriots and led the charge herself. Although the Dutch kept the Spaniards from taking Haarlem, troops surrounded the city. After a dreadful seven-month siege, the starving locals surrendered, followed by the kind of deplorable aftermath you can read about in any newspaper today.

Five years later, however, Haarlemers won their city back. Kenau received special kudos for her take-charge actions in the city's defense—an honor this Dutch treat relished until her death in her 60s. This being Holland, Kenau and her "Amazon battalion" were given pictorial immortality by local artists.

The Original Roaring Girl

er rap sheet was a mile long, her personal habits left a lot to be desired, and her aliases included Moll Cutpurse and the Roaring Girle. Who was she? Just the most unrepentant female crook and cutup England ever had, that's who. The English love an all-arounder, and **Moll Frith** didn't disappoint. Born about 1589, Frith got her first nickname from her talent for robbing pedestrians by cutting their purse strings. It soon became evident to admiring bystanders that this hard-drinking gal with a penchant for pipe tobacco and men's breeches would become a Renaissance woman of crime.

She wasn't merely into misdemeanors, however. When Moll reached her 40s, the British got into a civil war between the king and the Parliament. A rabid royal partisan, Moll took a hands-on part in the Great Rebellion, as it was called, by working as a highwayperson. In this capacity, on one famous occasion she whopped the daylights out of the commander-in-chief of the Parliamentary forces and his flunkies. After her first flush of patriotism, Ms. Cutpurse remembered she had a living to make—so she lightened the commander's load by 250 gold pieces. Moll got away clean; eventually, however, the livid commander caught her, and it was into the slammer. Not to worry, luv. Ever-thrifty Frith had enough put by to bribe her way to freedom, to the tune of 2,000 pounds.

When she'd had her fill of war and glory, Moll got serious about her work, establishing a huge network of thieves. To handle the end results more efficiently, she set up a pawnshop business whose recycled contents were hotter than a Thai curry. When robbery turned humdrum, Moll would do a gig as a forger or a fortune-teller. Sometimes she would serve a spell in Newgate, London's big prison. She didn't forget her friends in the joint, either, when she was out. On Sundays, Frith often spent part of her ill-gotten gains on food for the prisoners. (In those days, English prisons allowed you to deliver.)

But a steady diet of crime makes anyone a dull delinquent, Moll believed. Her sexual escapades were numerous. Judging by her happy-go-lucky choice of partners, she may have been lesbian or bisexual. With her flair for the dramatic, Ms. Frith also plunged into the theater, supposedly becoming the first female to appear on the Elizabethan stage. In her role as a cavalier, she pretty much played herself, wearing a doublet and singing a few off-color songs. Already notorious, Moll became famous—especially when diverse enchanted Englishmen wrote several more songs and plays about the urban Robina Hood with the heart of gold.

See here the Prefidesse o'th pilfring Trade
Mercuryes second, Venus's onely Mayd
Doublet and breeches in a Uniform dress e
The Female Hamar 1st a Kickshaw messe
Here no attraction that your fancy greets
Be't her FEATURES please not read her FEATS..

She looked straitlaced, but mischief-maker Moll was not.

In 1611, a comedy called *The Roaring Girle or Moll Cutpurse* opened at the Fortune stage in London. That same year, Moll got arrested in Saint Paul's cathedral for wearing men's clothing—which goes to show that even a celebrity couldn't pursue her eccentricities in peace. But she kept trying: Moll lived to a strenuous 75 and would probably still be sending London cops up in smoke, if she hadn't dropped of the dropsy.

Too Popular to Let Women Play

In the fourth and fifth centuries around the Mediterranean, a musical theater and dance form called pantomime shot to the top of the charts. Eleven centuries later, in the Far East, a similar evolution in entertainment took place—spearheaded by a Japanese woman named **Izumo no Okuni**. A dancer and religious drama performer, Okuni got involved in a benefit to rebuild a famous shrine and ended up touring with a company to raise money. On the road, she connected with a well-known comic, shared her ideas of melding mime and religious drama with him, and came up with Kabuki, the most popular genre of Japanese theater for the past 400 years. Not long after that, Okuni teamed up with a samurai who added his knowledge of classical drama to her inventive idea.

This dancer-choreographer also started the Kabuki tradition of males playing female roles, and vice versa. Oh, how that woman could swash a buckle! Her adoring public and the Japanese royals loved her trademark attire, a black priest's robe and a couple of swords in her belt. Although Kabuki is still wowing audiences in Japan, its founder Okuni wouldn't even be able to get on stage nowadays—male actors now play all the roles.

They Really Knew the Score

I taly, the land of the aria, was a congenial home for female composers. While dozens composed professionally, three got extraordinary recognition in Renaissance times.

Adopted by a rich banker of Venice, her mom a house servant, the possibly illegitimate **Barbara Strozzi** got a head start in music from her musically talented dad, Giulio. In the early 1600s, when she was barely 12, Barbara sang with a musical group that met at the Strozzi mansion. She started composing in her 20s, publishing madrigals, motets, and arias. After her father died, this singular single went professional, composing for affluent patrons and performing her own compositions. Barbara's voice must have been exceptional; her compositions (more than 50 still exist) were designed to showcase a lyrical soprano voice.

Born about 1540, singer **Maddalena Messari Casulana** also wrote madrigals. In her 40-some years, she composed a three-volume collection of 66 madrigals—the first published by any woman. A sparkling and confident musician, Maddalena didn't think of herself as the exception to the rule. She once wrote to a patron: "I want to show the world the foolish error of men, who so greatly believe themselves to be the masters of high intellectual gifts that cannot, it seems to them, be equally common among women."

A third female composer of note—and notoriety—was **Tarquinia Molza,** who wrote for the harp, viol, lute, and voice, and conducted as well. She possessed a soprano as brilliant as Venetian glass. Italy and Europe could be a tough sell when it came to female voices; by the 1500s, the royal courts reserved their most fulsome kudos for the surgery-enhanced male castrati singers. When Tarquinia came along in 1570 or so, her powerful voice cut through, if you'll pardon the expression, the castrati fad and stirred the public fancy. Established at the court of a duchess, her career *fortissimo*, Molza looked like a diva for the ages when disaster hit, in the form of a love affair with the wrong man. Exit Molza, *molto allegro*.

Unsung Elizabethans

 n 1537, an Englishwoman named **Katherine Champernowne Ashley** became governess to a frail four-year-old, who fondly called her "Kat." Instead of pampering her young charge, who was the daughter of King Henry VIII, Kat gave her an intellectual workout in math, astronomy, history, and geography. Instead of recess, Kat had her studying five languages. Before long, Princess Elizabeth could write letters to her half-brother Edward—in Latin! What Kat gave the child was worth more than Latin lessons, however. She provided unstinting love and stability. Kat was there to offer comfort during the revolving-door years of Henry's wives (and the horrific beheadings of Elizabeth's mom, Anne Boleyn, and her stepmother, Catherine Howard). Kat even endured a stretch in the Tower of London during the conspiratorial craziness of Bloody

Mary, Elizabeth's other half-sibling. In her mid-50s, Ashley finally saw "her" queen begin her triumphant solo reign.

During her terrifying childhood, **Elizabeth I** also had a second Rock of Gibraltar, **Blanche Parry**, who rocked her cradle, taught her Welsh, and guarded the girl as she grew. Both women devoted their lives to the luminescent girl in their care, who became the greatest career woman England ever had. What grand service they rendered; without them, it's hard to imagine a child withstanding that abuse and tragedy unscathed. When she took the throne, Elizabeth honored these fiercely faithful companions who'd seen her through the worst of times. Governess Kat became the First Lady of the Bedchamber; Blanche Parry, the Keeper of the Royal Jewels and Books.

As she grew to maturity, Elizabeth gained royal presence. From her father, she inherited brains, boldness, theatrical gold-red hair, milky pale skin, and long fingers. From the ghastly fates of her mother and her stepmother, both killed before

Liz loved wild dancing, her water closet, and her women companions.

her eighth birthday, Elizabeth gained a grim determination to stay independent. She would string along male admirers and suitors, flirt, perhaps even love. But marry? Never.

The year Elizabeth became queen, at age 25, a council memo bemoaned England's status: "The realm is exhausted; steadfast enemies, but no steadfast friends." In her 45-year reign, Elizabeth gradually brought back prosperity, although it took 15 years to pay off the debts left by Papa. She brought about peace by ending a war with France, and later whipped the "invincible" Spanish Armada. And she brought about a golden age of literature, drama, and the arts.

This tall Tudor adored fresh flowers, fireworks, the theater, the smell of vanilla (she put it on everything), archery, and wild dancing. Unlike other Elizabethans, she hated unwashed bodies and bad smells. In 1597 her godson got on her good side forever when he invented the water closet and installed one for her.

Near the end of her long reign, good Queen Bess said: "Though God has raised me high, yet I count the glory of my crown that I have reigned with your loves. I do not so much rejoice that God has made me a Queen, as to be a Queen over so thankful a people." That love—from Kat Ashley, Blanche Parry, and the English multitudes—was amply reciprocated. Seldom has a ruler been as well-loved and as competent a leader as this queen who gave her name to an entire era.

Angelic Lust at the Nunnery

 *bambina* of nine when she entered the humblest nunnery in Pescia, Italy, **Benedetta Carlini** became its youngest abbess—and no wonder. Besides management skills and cajoling talents that kept the convent's cash flow positive, she had divine gifts as a mystic. Benedetta predicted the future, declaring that a plague would hit Pescia in 1631, for instance. She had long conversations with male angels. Her forehead and hands regularly bled (a phenomenon called stigmata). She went into trances on command. Eventually she reported that she had exchanged hearts with Jesus. Later, she

"married" Christ in a special ceremony attended by a few select guests. The abbess, however, really pushed the spiritual envelope when she foretold her own death, "died," and returned with orders for her nuns along the lines of, "I can get you into Paradise ... probably ... if you do exactly as I say."

In 1622, the church sent officials to investigate Benedetta's showy claims. During the course of the investigation, their interviews turned up more surprising tidbits. The abbess had an almost demonic craving for Italian salami, one nun tattled. The abbess helped along her stigmata with a large needle, another keyhole-peeper reported. But the biggest throat-grabber was the news that Sister Benedetta had a sex life as intense and splashy as her spiritual one. Nun **Bartolomea Crivelli** revealed that she and the abbess had had a two-year, three-times-a-week affair—not that she liked it, the young canary hastily added.

In medieval Europe, lesbian sexuality didn't exist (at least in the minds of males). To describe the acts that took place between the lusty abbess and young Bartolomea, the horrified clergy resorted to phrases like "mutual corruption." (During the juicier bits, the scribe taking it down got so shaken that his calligraphy became almost illegible!)

When confronted with the nun's story, the nimble-tongued abbess gave a politician's glib response: "I have no recollection—it musta been that angel Splenditello." Indeed, all the nuns said that when the abbess hit her stride with an angelic vision, her voice deepened and her face took on the expression of a male teen. Psychologically this made sense; becoming a horny male angel allowed Benedetta to create an identity that fit into—and made an end run around—the values of her patriarchal society.

After wrenching thought, church investigators gave the abbess a break: She'd evidently been possessed by the devil and thus wasn't fully accountable for her actions. (Unlike witchcraft, possession was considered involuntary.) Instead of a date with a bonfire, Benedetta got locked in a convent cell for 35 years. Evidently perceived as the innocent victim in the situation, Bartolomea, the young squealer, remained a nun at Pescia.

Although neither nuns nor locals protested her harsh treatment, Benedetta kept her standing as a visionary—especially after she hit the mark with the plague prediction. Benedetta even scored a final posthumous triumph. Unconcerned about her sex life, faithful fans flocked to the chapel to touch her body or, better yet, steal a relic from the holy woman they thought of as a confidant of angels.

Fight or Be Eaten

Women conducted high-level negotiations in Africa during the 1600s? That was child's play for **Nzinga Mbande**, the king's sister and official in charge of forging a lasting peace between the slave-rich land of Ndongo (known today as Angola) and Portugal, its slave-hungry colonizer. Naturally, the white guys tried a few psychological ploys, thinking they would rattle and/or humiliate this African arbitrator. Once they brought Nzinga to where their governor was seated but neglected to put out a chair for her. Instead of protesting, she ordered one of her slaves to get on his hands and knees; sitting on the back of this human chair, she wheeled and dealed all day. (Some accounts say that after the meeting, Nzinga toyed further with European minds by having Mr. Chair executed on the spot.)

When the official bickering was done, Nzinga liked nothing better than to kick back with a personal concubator or two. It was an article of faith among Ngolans—at least those with tons of status—that you can never have too many concubators, the male equivalent of the more familiar concubine or palace mistress. The 50-odd concubators in Nzinga's harem answered to female names and dressed fit to kill in feminine finery.

In 1624, Nzinga's brother was bumped off, and she became queen. After she filled her cabinet with women, the Portuguese broke the peace treaty. With a sigh of relish, Nzinga threw off her diplomatic posture and prepared her troops for war. Believing that females shouldn't get just the cushy desk jobs, the queen called up women as well as men for the armed forces. To lead her warriors, she and her two fierce sisters, Kifunji and Mukumbu, wore matching animal-skin outfits and carried personal arsenals of sword, ax, and bow and arrows. By this time, Nzinga and family had also called it quits with the Christianity imported by the Portuguese and went back to good ole ritual cannibalism.

Although Kifunji was killed in battle, Nzinga and Mukumbu really got into the spirit of things, continuing to fight the Portuguese until the late 1650s. As you might expect, the prospect of being the object of ritual cannibalism had a negative effect on Portuguese morale. In addition, Nzinga had the bright idea of attacking and conquering other African kingdoms, which allowed her to build a confederacy (however involuntary) big enough to beat the enemy. She also formed alliances with the Dutch, intending to move against them once she'd gotten the other Europeans out of her hair.

In 1659, this spirited leader finally signed a treaty of peace and friendship with the Europeans she had fought for 35 years. An African queen to the last, Nzinga lived into her 80s—still bright-eyed and fond of noshing on human flesh now and then. All the attention lavished by those concubators must have done its job. Even today, Nzinga's nifty deeds are remembered (and the gorier ones glossed over) in the history books of Angolan schoolchildren. After Angola regained its independence in the 20th century, grateful citizens named a boulevard in the capital after her.

How Quinine Got to the Old World

ife before quinine was really dire all over mosquito-infested South America, so **Ana de Osorio**, Countess of Chinchon, wasn't all that tickled when her husband came home in 1630 with a new assignment: "Honey, I'm the new viceroy in charge of running Peru. We'll be leaving Spain for lovely Lima."

A few bug-filled months later, a vast amount of shivering was taking place. Both the countess and the viceroy came down with malaria and tertian fever. None of Ana's home remedies had any effect. Desperate, the countess decided to try a local cure. Soon, bands of Peruvians were beating the bushes, looking for a certain tree they just knew was around the rain forest somewhere. When they finally located a specimen, the bark's miracle antimalarial alkaloid, quinine, put Ana and the viceroy on the mend in no time.

In 1640, the diplomats returned to Spain. Always thinking ahead, Ana threw some quinine bark, just in case, in her carry-on luggage—and a smooth move it turned out to be. Spain happened to be in the midst of a malaria epidemic, and, boy, did the countess look good after dosing locals with her personal stash. It soon got dubbed "the contessa's powder," and Ana's deeds were raved about in print.

The most lasting tribute, however, came about a century after Ana had brought quinine from the New World to the Old. Swedish botanist Carolus Linnaeus developed the Latin-naming scheme for plants and animals; when he got to the quinine-producing tree, he gave the genus name *Chinchona* to nearly 160 species of trees in honor of the clever Countess of Chinchon.

Portrait of a killer.

England's First Avon Lady

A careerwoman with calves of iron, **Joan Dant** pioneered the door-to-door sales pitch in 17th-century England. Her peddler prowess became famous in London and environs—where working conditions included grouchy dogs, no sidewalks, filthy cobblestones, and flying chamberpots.

Only after becoming a weaver's widow did Mrs. Dant decide to become a traveling entrepreneur. She started with socks, then built up her inventory to carry a whole line of hosiery and haberdashery.

Joan Dant was Quaker by faith, and the honesty of her business dealings—and the great networking she did among fellow Quakers—soon made her the peddler to watch. In time, Dant enterprises went international. Modest by nature, and a thrift queen at heart, Joan schlepped her wares to faraway Paris and Brussels, all the while amassing the Renaissance equivalent of money market funds.

Thanks to her daily cardiovascular workouts, she didn't perish until age 84. At that time, sorrowing friends and startled beneficiaries found that the dauntless marathoner was worth a small fortune. Most of the 9,000 pounds and other assets she left went to Quaker widows and fatherless children. As Joan put it, "I got it by the rich and I mean to leave it to the poor."

Her Brains Saved Rembrandt's Bacon

Like many painters, Rembrandt van Rijn was a Dutch master at the "I'm just so bad with money" shtick. Luckily, he had a gal pal in a million, the redoubtable **Hendrickje Stoffels**. After becoming a widower, Mr. R. played house with his son's nanny, who brought a breach-of-promise suit. Stoffels stepped in, giving testimony that got him off the marital hook. She took on the job of mothering his small son, Titus, later becoming that staple of starving artists, the muse/model/mistress. In 1654, she shyly announced, "A little artist is on the way," hoping to get a more binding offer. Instead, she got slammed with a fine and public repentance for the sin of fornication by church authorities.

Rembrandt, in dire need of the income stream from his late wife's will, refused to remarry. With a sigh, Hendrickje had baby Cornelia and kept on modeling and keeping house for Mr. Hapless.

Rembrandt's model, mistress, money manager.

Although it might seem hard to see how Rembrandt's financial situation could have worsened, in 1658, it did. The painter went bankrupt; the $65,000 house he'd bought with first wife, Saskia, the antiques, and the art were auctioned for a pittance. At this point, problem-solver Hendrickje went into partnership with 17-year-old Titus. In an artful ploy that would move the IRS to tears, their enterprise shielded Mr. R. from his creditors while allowing him to work as an employee of the H&T art dealership. Thanks to his mistress and his son, Rembrandt had breathing room to produce his most powerful works.

With this kind of stress, it's no wonder Hendrickje died young. At least, however, our single mom and volunteer stepmom left a legacy that few could top: a series of exquisite paintings of her by Rembrandt, who clearly did love this woman who shared his life for 20 years. The surviving paintings, including the magical *Woman Bathing in a Stream*, are considered by many to be the most touching works in the artist's huge oeuvre.

Playful Adventurer

From debtors' prison to deafening applause as the first female playwright to get her works on England's version of Broadway, **Aphra Amis Behn** came a long way, baby. Her story began in Surinam, of all places, where Aphra spent her youth in the sticky tropics of South America. Eventually she married a Mr. Behn and the couple headed for London in 1665—jolly bad timing, given it was the year of the Great Plague. Behn promptly expired, leaving Aphra unmerry and broke.

Résumé in hand, Aphra hit up King Charles of England (who had a small war going with the Dutch) for an espionage job. Delighted, the king sent her to Holland, where bilingual Behn uncovered a plot: The Dutch planned to sail up the Thames and set fire to the English fleet! "Well, isn't that special?" said the king, failing to heed (or pay) her.

Aphra was starting to get down on men as providers or employers. To finish her spy assignment, what could she do but borrow money for expenses? On her return to London, agent Behn got grim news: Not only did the damned Brits refuse to cover her costs, she got tossed in debtors' prison by her creditor!

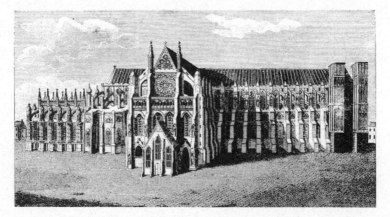

Westminster Abbey, where Aphra is buried.

The Poets' Corner in Westminster, where Aphra should have landed.

She did get an "I told you so" out of the deal; in June 1667, 17 Dutch warships attacked an unprepared England, making King Charles the laughingstock of Europe.

Now rotting away in a festering hole, Mrs. B. rethought her career goals. By the time she got released, she had her first risqué play roughed out. By 1670, audiences were splitting their sides over her witty works. Lines like "Come away! Poverty's catching!" made her famous.

Besides her 20 plays, Aphra composed poetry, wrote 14 novels, and did translations into French (with a time-out here and there for a liaison, one of which came with a bonus of syphilis). Hailed as the first woman in England to earn a living by writing, she was also the first English author to express sympathy for slaves. In one of her books, this racy Renaissance role model defined herself by saying, "I had rather die in the adventure of noble achievements, than live in obscure and sluggish security." In her 50 far-from-sluggish years, Aphra won honors and left a wealth of writings (if not money). She was buried in prestigious Westminster Abbey, though in the actresses' section, rather than her rightful place in Poets' Corner.

Black Hats
Beware

Some called this English blueblood "My lady." To lowlifes and villains, however, **Anne Clifford** was Sheriff Anne. As a teen, she'd inherited the badge from her pop, the Earl of Cumberland—but first had to fight against male relatives, a messy will, and other obstacles. Four decades passed before she was able to take office.

By that time, Anne was superbly equipped to deal with varmints—starting with her husband, the Earl of Dorset. When she became the richest heiress in England, he tried to get that lovely lucre converted to spending cash by various underhanded means. He did not prevail, as Anne's own diary showed.

In 1650, Anne finally moseyed up to northwestern England for her official swearing-in. Four times a year, she entertained the area justices of

Plenty of perps for this lady sheriff—including her husband.

the peace, riding a white stallion to greet them. Anne Clifford faithfully served as sheriff until her death in 1676, signing writs, reporting on election results, making public proclamations from the king and queen—and keeping black hats and greedy husbands out of Westmorland.

When not busy upholding the law, Anne also founded hospitals, restored castles, and built homes for the poor.

Preacher, Prisoner, Warden?

lthough **Margaret Fell** and company called themselves the Society of Friends, they soon got labeled "quakers" for their go-to-meeting style, described in an indignant 1655 pamphlet as "Shriekings, shakings, quakings, roarings, yellings, howlings, tremblings in the bowels, and risings in the bellies."

Margaret's bowel-trembling came in midlife. A silver-spoon child born in England, at 16 she married more money and had seven brilliant daughters and a son. In her 30s, she came down with a case of spiritual acid indigestion. Then she heard Quaker leader George Fox speak, and an inner light came on. Stunned by her insta-conversion, her husband refused to shriek, quake, or join—but didn't fight her choice.

Within six years, Margaret was a widow and a big wheel in the Friends. Nicknamed the Nursing Mother of Quakerism, she kept the finances going, plagued the royals with unsolicited books and letters, and filled in whenever Fox and others were in prison or abroad (a weekly occurrence, by the sound of it). At her Swarthmoor Hall, she built a tradition of philanthropy that became a hallmark of the society.

I want to shimmy like my sister Margaret.

In 1664, the widow Fell was charged with holding illegal meetings. After refusing to take a court oath, and threatened with a life sentence and seizure of her property, she calmly said, "If the king's pleasure is to take my estate, on account of my conscience, and not for any evil or wrong done, let him do as he pleaseth."

He pleaseth, and she was promptly locked into leaky Lancaster Castle, where George Fox was already serving time (again). Instead of working on her bench-pressing, Mrs. Fell sat down and wrote the first of 16 books and pamphlets. *Women's Speaking* was published in 1666; due to leg irons, Fell was unable to do an author tour. She remained behind bars until 1668.

At 55, Fell married Fox, delighting everyone except his daughter and her son—who teamed up for a vendetta against the newlyweds. In 1670, they managed to get Margaret returned to jail! Thanks to lobbying from Quaker preacher **Elizabeth Hooton,** Margaret was made an overseer at Fleet prison, and got to give perks (like regular meals) to inmates. (Strange as it sounds to modern ears, in Renaissance times many jailers were former inmates.)

By now the Quaker movement had grown huge. Antiwar and pro-simplicity, the Society of Friends also empowered women; more than 200 became preachers in the 1600s.

Margaret lived longer than 80 years, arguing to the last that the voice women had gained among the Friends was proof of a new millennium and "the True Church."

Coming Out of the Armoire

Because of laws making lesbianism as felonious as intimacy with barnyard animals, there just weren't that many "I'm out!" parties in Renaissance centuries, even in oh-so-erotic France.

So the public actions of **Julie d'Aubigny de Maupin**—to say nothing of what she did behind closed doors—furnished considerable fuel for outrage in the late 1600s. Supposedly born poor, the beauteous Aubigny clawed her way out of the gutter into the Paris Opera, becoming a contralto singer. Equally marvelous was her way with a sword, another useful skill when you're clawing your way out of the gutter.

Ze women, zey go mad for my fake goatee—touché!

After a performance, there was nothing that La Maupin liked better than to throw on her favorite leisure wear—that of a fashionable French cavalier—and go kick some serious male derrière in a back alley. In her most notorious duel, at a ball thrown by the king, she took on three male opponents who'd gotten riled when she passionately kissed "their" girl on the dance floor. Interrupted in mid-osculation, Maupin puffed out her chest and said, "You wanna piece a me?" She either whipped the trio or killed them. Since dueling was a felony within the city limits, she could have been in *très* deep trouble; but the king was amused by La Maupin's attitude and panache, and let her off.

On stage, Aubigny often took male roles, using her dueling abilities. So rapid was her rapier that audiences found it hard to believe Aubigny was female; on one occasion, she had to go topless temporarily to prove it.

A woman of great passions for any gender, she dazzled and won a variety of females. One piquant caper was her runaway affair with a nun from Avignon, who crawled back to her convent, utterly spent, three months later. That little stunt earned Aubigny a felony sentence, later commuted, to be burned at the stake. But La Maupin kept on pushing the outrage envelope. In Marseilles, her masterful performance as a male cavalier stunned a young fan, who ran off with her post-opera. This episode probably wouldn't have attracted that much notice, except the fan was a fat-cat merchant's daughter. To avoid a lesbian/antisodomy bonfire, the runaway later claimed to have blown the whistle on Maupin "just as soon as I discovered her gender, your honor."

On this charge, Aubigny went to jail and had a prime seat on death row. Luckily, audiences in Paris and elsewhere fancied the diva so much that public clamor overturned her sentence. From that point on, jaded authorities said, *"C'est la vie"* to Maupin's subsequent high jinks, no matter how flamboyant or outré.

To Be or Not to Be (Leered At)

n English actress famed for playing Roxelana (the real-life harem beauty who'd become the first Sultana), **Hester Davenport** had a big fan base. Filthy-rich admirer Lord Oxford, for instance, often dropped hints about "taking care of her." Despite her lousy pay, Hester merely smiled. Oxford threw gifts, favors, and love spells her way, with no results. Finally he brought up the m-word: marriage.

Then Oxford did some play-acting himself, since tying the knot with an actress was still a class A felony in the 1660s. He arranged a bogus ceremony, with musicians standing in as minister and witnesses. (The cake may have been real, though.) After their wedding night, Oxford awoke Hester with the tender words,

"I'll call ya!" Now aware that her marriage was a sham, Hester snatched up her fake husband's all-too-genuine sword and ran him through. After his wound healed, they continued as a couple until a child materialized a few years later, whereupon Hester took her paternity grievance to the king. Besides a fat pension, the actress won the right to call herself the Countess of Oxford—*even* after she married another aristocrat.

Hester enjoyed a happy ending, but the 80 or more actresses active in the English theater between 1660 and 1689 often got sexually harassed, on the job and off. **Rebecca Marshall**, for instance, had to obtain a restraining order from the king against a fan, who then hired a thug to pelt Rebecca with excrement on her way home!

Although theater management had rules forbidding backstage visitors, males ignored them entirely. Even leading ladies such as **Elizabeth Barry** and **Anne Bracegirdle** found themselves dressing (and undressing) in front of uninvited male eyes.

Bracegirdle, noted for tragic and comic roles, kept mum about her private life. Barry, acknowledged as the top dramatic actress of her day, did likewise. She even achieved a piece of the action, owning shares in the second company she helped form. Except for the occasional snog with a titled honey, hardheaded Barry stayed single and solo—a state of affairs that earned her vicious character attacks. Unlike physical abuse and prying eyes, such attacks were mere words, the raw material that Barry worked with every day.

To date me, start with a good grovel. And a ring.

The Musical Prodigies of Venice

Who says that illegitimate girl children couldn't get a break in Renaissance Italy? In Venice they could. For centuries, four imposing *ospedali* (hospitals with orphanages attached) took in foundlings and trained hundreds of girls to be classical musicians, vocalists, music copyists, and composers. (Youngsters who couldn't carry a note in a bucket were taught an array of other useful jobs and skills.)

Lacking last names, the girls got musical handles or took the name of their *ospedale*. For example, **Prudenza dal Contralto** sang. **Maddalena dal Violin** played fiddle. **Zabetta of the Incurabili** was a warbler from the Hospital for the Incurables. Concerts at the Pietà, most famous of the four orphanages, featured a full orchestra and chorus.

The glitterati of Venice attended the Saturday, Sunday, and holiday performances, the ticket revenues going

Tuneful team: composer Vivaldi and his orphan girls.

to support the orphanages. One awestruck attendee described his night at the Pietà: "They sing like angels, and play violin, flute, oboe, organ, cello, and bassoon, not even stopping at the largest instruments. Some 40 girls perform at each concert. There is no more delightful sight than a pretty young nun wearing a white robe and a bouquet of pomegranate flowers in her hair. . . . The lightness of attack and the purity of tone of their voices is simply divine."

This delighted concertgoer may have let his imagination

overheat: The girls weren't nuns, they wore robes or dresses of various colors, and they couldn't be seen—most audiences simply heard them play behind screens of wrought-iron and gauze. The discipline they got did resemble that of a convent, however, and included fines and even hair chopping for tardiness and other sins.

Musical training started very early for promising nightingales. After the youngsters became oldsters, they could continue as musicians. Although legally they were indentured servants of Venice, the women earned modest incomes and could bequeath it as they liked. If an *ospedale* girl wanted to marry, she got a dowry. If she chose to enter a nunnery, she could.

Many became virtuosas, famous far beyond Venice. Visitors to the city knew that if you hadn't been to an *ospedale* performance, you hadn't done Venice. Fans argued over favorites, comparing **Margarita from the Mendicanti** to Zabetta, who had a violinlike quality to her voice.

The girls were taught by the finest musicians of the day, who vied for these well-paid positions. One who spent 40 years as a teacher-musician at the Ospedale della Pietà was Antonio Vivaldi, whose musical compositions (notably *The Four Seasons*) are evergreen. For the listener today, his music gains depth and poignancy when you realize how much of it was written for the tender voices and young fingers of talented orphaned girls. The grand structures of Venice's *ospedali* are no more, but a small museum dedicated to their marvelous musical legacy is located near the spot where the Pietà once stood. If only today's movers and shakers would have the good sense to emulate such a stellar idea.

House rules: Arrive late for aria practice, get a bad haircut.

PART FOUR

UPPITY WOMEN

OF THE

New World

LATE 1500s–1899

✳ ✳ ✳ ✳ ✳ ✳ ✳

*Sea travel stinks! This New World
better be good.*

Very Early Americans

Who was the first English child born on North American soil? That would be **Virginia Dare**, whose mother, Eleanor, brought her into a risky New World on August 18, 1587. The baby popped out at the Virginia Colony (also in its infancy) on Roanoke Island, today in North Carolina. When baby Ginny was nine days old, her grandfather, John White, leader of this hapless band of would-be colonists, hightailed it back to England for desperately needed supplies. What with wars, sponsor bankruptcy, and so on, he didn't return until August 1590. By then the Roanoke settlement, the white colonists, and baby Virginia had vanished. Their fate remains an eerie mystery. Newborn Dare, however, did win a certain immortality; the island and the nearby mainland are called Dare County in her honor.

Rotten luck and poor planning also dogged three shiploads of English colonists, all male, who settled on a mosquito-rich, brackish river island they dubbed Jamestown. A year later, in 1608, two rashly eager women arrived: **Ann Margaret Forrest** and her maid, **Anna Burras**, accompanied by Forrest's husband. Life at Jamestown was no cabaret. Fire destroyed the colony's first fort and the food supply, and the colonists owed their survival to the kindly acts of Pocahontas and other members of the local American Indian tribes. Modern archaeologists have found Mrs. Forrest's remains, and a 3-D model of her head has been made from a CAT scan of her skull. Through their detective work we know that she ate bread made from Old World wheat. It's likely that bad drinking water and the so-called Starving Time in the winter of 1609–10 carried her off. When she died, her 4-foot 8-inch frame was interred in a posh, gabled coffin. The longer-lived Anna Burras garnered a first of her own: At age 14, she married a surviving colonist named John Laydon. Their English wedding was the first ever celebrated on these shores.

A longer life and a happier fate awaited new colonist **Mary Allerton** in 1620. The weary four-year-old gazed over the rail of the *Mayflower* at the landscape of Plymouth, Massachusetts. After the stormy misery of a two-month voyage, land must have looked awfully good. It was November, however, and half of her companions, including her mother, would perish before spring.

Of Dutch heritage, Mary became a founding foremother. Seven of her eight children survived, as the settlement thrived. The longest lived of the *Mayflower's* passengers, Mary witnessed the founding of 12 of the 13 original colonies.

Nice Natives Finish Last

"White people—what a pain," thought **Wetamo**, a heavy hitter of the Wampanoag tribe. Her father-in-law had kept one stinking band of Puritans alive through the winter of 1621, and then they spread like crabgrass. From a leadership clan herself, Wetamo wed Wamsutta, the son of a major chief. After the honeymoon, the two Ws settled in Pokanoket, the main village of the Wampanoags, to run things.

By 1662, however, the peace between natives and newcomers was sadly frayed. The whites kept naming and claiming stuff. "Oh, you're squatting on our new colony of Rhode Island," they would say, pointing to Wetamo's village and anything else that wasn't nailed down.

Then came the day when whites dragged her husband away for interrogation, and he ended up dead. At that point, Wetamo became sachem, or chief, with 300 warriors at her disposal. For a whole decade, she kept her temper, and the peace, while her brother-in-law Metacomet (whom the native language–phobic Puritans called King Philip) tried to make sense of the whites' demands.

Their forbearance was to no avail. Finally, in 1675, Wetamo and Metacomet joined forces in a resistance movement called King Philip's War. Talk about a traumatic conflict: Wetamo went through two more husbands during this period. She also had to deal with white POWs, including the contentious **Mary Rowlandson**. Unused to being bossed by either Native Americans or women, Mary made a terrible captive, and after 83 days was cashed in for 20 pounds of goods. The tribe even threw in some tobacco, as a "We'll pay you wampum to take her" gesture.

Relieved to unload the Rowlandson problem, Wetamo went into battle, easily wiping out Lancaster, Massachusetts, and other areas. All told, her warriors destroyed 20 towns in New England and killed about 600 colonists. Nevertheless, the game went to the whites. By the summer of 1676, more than 5,000 men had been killed or taken to the West Indies as slaves.

Wetamo may have died by drowning; postmortem, though, worse things may have happened. One account of the period says that Native American prisoners saw her head displayed on a pole, and "made a horrible and diabolical lamentation, crying out that it was their Queen." A sorry end indeed for a proud and intelligent woman, who had pursued peaceful coexistence until no options were left.

Health Heroine

ext May 26, why don't we honor **Lady Mary Wortley Montagu**? She's the 18th-century Englishwoman who singlehandedly saved thousands from what was then a fate worse than death: smallpox (called "small" to distinguish it from the great pox, syphilis.)

Early in her marriage, smallpox struck 25-year-old Mary. She had the type called *confluent*; the pocks ran together in one huge sore, leaving her ruined face covered with deep reddish craters. When she first saw herself in the mirror, she wrote a mocking poem: "Alas, how am I grown/A frightful spectre to myself unknown!" Smallpox had disfigured her but failed to destroy her zest for living. (She would also leave the world a legacy of spirited writings from poetry to travel essays.)

Seven years later, living with her children and ambassador husband in Turkey and mingling with local women, Lady Mary observed the Ottoman Empire custom of inoculation (also known as variolation) against smallpox, with tiny amounts of the live virus. As time would show, the procedure had one draw-

Turkish women taught her how to inoculate.

back: It could bring on the disease in about 3 percent of those inoculated. Still, it seemed miraculous to Montagu, compared to the numbers killed by smallpox (30 to 40 percent)—plus the countless blinded and severely scarred survivors. Inoculation also gave lifetime immunity; that was important, because small-pox epidemics returned again and again.

When Mary returned to England in 1719, she brought the method back and fought fiercely for its acceptance. By inoculating her own children, she convinced the royal family to do the same. Many doctors rejected variolation—and female impertinence. Even after broader acceptance, medical professionals inflicted more risk and pain by adding lengthy courses of purging and blood-letting to the process.

It would be another 80 years before Edward Jenner developed vaccination, a method that carried much less risk. During those decades, smallpox jumped the Atlantic, bringing epidemics to the New World in 1721, 1729, 1751, and 1774–76. During the last of these epidemics, inoculation probably saved the lives of Ben Franklin, Thomas Jefferson, John Adams, and the signers of the Declaration of Independence. George Washington, who had survived smallpox in 1751, inoculated his entire Continental Army. It's horrifying to imagine what the fledgling colonies would have done without Lady Mary's solution, which was the only defense at that time against the world's longest-lived killer. Since its first recorded appearance circa 1350 B.C., experts estimate that smallpox has killed more humans than all plagues and wars combined.

Lawyer–Land Baron Dream Team

 n English Catholic family rolling in assets and arrogance, the Brents—two brothers and two sisters, **Margaret Brent** and **Mary Brent**—arrived in the Maryland Colony in 1638. Founded by fellow Catholic Lord Baltimore, at that time the

Hey, thou! Which way's the courtroom?

colony had only a few hundred settlers huddled on its shores. For the well-to-do the juicy enticements to colonize included land grants for anyone who paid ship's passage and maintenance for able-bodied males to work the land. Margaret and Mary quickly established Sisters Freehold, raising livestock and adding new chunks of real estate by bringing over as many nicely buffed indentured male servants as they could.

By 1646, life in the colony had turned more precarious. Having a keen legal mind as well as business sense, Margaret had already won the confidence of (and the power of attorney for) Lord Baltimore and his brother, Lord Calvert, who both served as colony governors. As their legal representative, she collected rents and paid their debts. Now she stepped up to quell a rebellion, restoring order by feeding the colony's soldiers, unpaid and hungry. Chaos averted, she marched into the Maryland Assembly session and said, "You need to let me do as you chaps do, and vote. I'll need to get two votes, however—one as your major landowner, and another as Lord Baltimore's attorney." By this time, Lord Calvert had expired, and the ungrateful new governor refused her request. Members of the Maryland Assembly, however, defended her stewardship, saying it was "better for the Colony's safety at that time in her hands than in any man's."

Nevertheless, Ms. Brent was denied. At this point, she did a pretty good imitation of Al Pacino in a courtroom by roaring, "Out of order! This governor is out of order! This *colony* is out of order!"

You won't be surprised to learn that combative Margaret filed more lawsuits than anyone else in the Maryland Colony. Only when her sister, Mary, died in 1658 did Margaret cease, choosing to move across Chesapeake Bay to found a community in the Virginia Colony. She called her new digs Peace. There she ruled the roost, a robust and independent single woman who continued to help her friends until she left this world at 71.

Salem's Satanic Sleepovers

Tituba, a household slave of Preacher Parris and his family, missed her Caribbean homeland during the frosty winters in Salem, Massachusetts. Between chores, Tituba entertained her owner's children, **Abigail** and **Betty Parris**, with tales of magic and superstition. Other neighborhood girls, mostly bored teenagers, came to listen to Tituba and her Barbados folklore.

This group of eight kids began to dabble in small sorceries, from palm reading to conjuring with scissors and a candle. Some, like **Ann Putnam**, a high-strung 12-year-old, dabbled more deeply, wanting to contact the spirits. These goings-on with Tituba remained secret for months. But the stress of doing what was a deadly sin in the eyes of Puritan grownups began to make the smaller girls sick. Their hysterics and convulsions quickly spread to the other girls. Some became physically ill.

The Massachusetts villagers of Salem were appalled. Charges began flying faster than a black mass–bound broomstick, with Preacher Parris leading the pack. Most of the supposedly bewitched girls ultimately gave testimony in court; Ann Putnam was especially verbal. When it came time for Tituba to testify, she said what everyone salivated to hear. Red cats and red rats talked to her, she said. There was a tall man and strange shapes that wanted her to pinch the children.

The good news: Missed the necktie party.

Dozens of accused women—including Tituba, a hard-of-hearing grandma named **Rebecca Nurse**, and a beggar named **Sarah Good**—were convicted of witchcraft. In 1692, 20 were hanged. Tituba, meanwhile, sat on death row for 13 months. The following year, the witch craze abating, she and others still incarcerated were released.

Tituba was then hit with a large invoice for jailhouse grub and her nights in the cell. Even though she had compelling reasons for nonpayment, the court was unwilling to accept them. Tituba found herself put up for resale at a slave auction to pay for her hoosegow B&B.

Other witchy activities took place during the same period. A gal named **Mercy Short** had gone with others to Boston Prison to peek at the accused Salem witches. While there, the

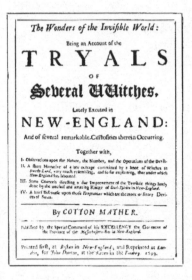

The bad news: Got sold down the river for debts.

accused Sarah Good asked her for tobacco, and Mercy made loud fun of her. On that day Mercy began to suffer diabolical visions.

Even after Sarah was hanged, Mercy received spectral visits. Her vivid descriptions, such as, "He was a short tawny man, with One Cloven Foot," had preacher Cotton Mather hanging on every word. During one of his sermons, Mercy fell into major convulsions. What with her devil-induced fits, and the congregation praying over her, and the appearance of "witches' marks" on her body,

Mercy was pretty busy—and the complete center of attention until the spring of 1693.

At that point, she became disappointingly normal. While Mather and congregation congratulated themselves, Mercy returned to housemaid work and took up more mundane activities, such as bar-hopping and fornicating. (You might think that Cotton and company would have stepped up the prayer vigils. But, no.) That bewitching, still inexplicable era in Massachusetts was over.

Must be true—it's in print: "Devil made her do it," says Cotton Mather.

Captured by Indians . . . or Rescued?

Born into a preacher's clan that was the leading family of Deerfield, Massachusetts, **Eunice Williams** led a privileged life until she was eight. Then, in a terrifying raid by Iroquois Mohawks, she, her family, and nearly a hundred neighbors were captured in 1704. Her mother died on the trek north to French Canada; her father and brother were ransomed, then tried for years to pay ransom to free Eunice.

All their efforts failed. Finally the Williamses learned the uncomfortable truth: Eunice didn't want to come back. Adopted by the tribe, she forgot English, married a Mohawk, and had several daughters. Perhaps the most ghastly part of the story from the Puritan point of view was that she had adopted Catholicism, too.

Eunice came to embrace the life of two adoptive cultures, Native American and French Catholic. Affectionately called by her Indian nickname, which meant "she brings in corn," she stood as godmother to both whites and Iroquois. She saw her daughters Marie and Catherine marry local chieftains, and lived to be 89.

The story of this unredeemed captive is fascinating for several reasons. During the United States' first 200 years, many females besides Eunice were kidnapped by Native Americans and refused to return to their own families and cultures. It's a penetrating and little-explored commentary on the role that women played—or were kept from playing—in white colonial society.

This sure beats the Puritan life.

Swashbuckling: Not as Easy as It Looks

 n the late 1600s, two girls born in the Old World met and became the New World's most-talked-about partners in crime.

Mary Read, encouraged from an early age by her mum and granny to shoplift and cross-dress, signed up for duty on a British man-of-war vessel. Once on board, Mary fell for fellow limey Jules, who took her gender outing in stride. Since they shared a passion for brews, they soon left the sea to open a tavern in Breda. Another dratted outbreak of peace killed business, however; and Jules responded to bankruptcy by dying. Mary, who thankfully had not taken her men's attire to Goodwill, headed for the West Indies on a merchant ship. In mid-voyage her vessel was commandeered by noted rascal Calico Jack and his pirates.

Meanwhile, carrot-topped **Anne Bonney** from County Cork found herself in the wilds of South Carolina, where her family had hastily emigrated after a lawyer-impregnates-housemaid scandal. Bonney quickly grew into a brawler who ran away early and coupled casually. Always interested in breaking more commandments,

Mary Read: not as innocent as she looked.

audacious Anne auditioned for the coveted job of pirate by stealing a ship and murdering its crew. "Hired!" said Calico Jack, her new employer.

Anne and Mary met on the poop deck of Calico Jack's ship, kindred spirits who soon saw they could become superbad in tandem. Both loved doing violence to ships, furniture, and other humans. To relax, now and again, the sexually spirited pair would jump the bones of some hottie they fancied.

The new gal pals worked nonstop to establish their vile reps on the bounding main. Thanks to them, their ship remained at the top of the most-wanted charts for three years in a row. But even highly motivated pirates get sloppy. In 1720 their ship was captured by the British Navy—a snap because the crew was intoxicated.

Anne Bonney: even less law-abiding.

Fuming at the others, Anne and Mary were taken in irons to Jamaica for trial, along with Calico Jack and the rest of the crew. Calico and company soon swung from a yardarm. The women, however, "pled their bellies," a useful but short-term ploy used by pregnant criminals to avoid the noose.

As pirates are notoriously lax at account-keeping, records are murky as to what happened to this high-seas Thelma and Louise. Mary Read seems to have died in prison or in childbirth. Anne, on the other hand, may have gotten away. For a time, her "wanted for murder" posters graced taverns throughout the New World, inspiring a whole new generation of ne'er-do-wells, male and female.

Gay Caballeras

ucky little orphan **Annie Lezama de Urinza**: In 17th-century Peru, she managed to find a congenial home with the de Sonza family, and in that well-heeled household, encountered a fellow mischief-maker in their daughter, **Eustaquia de Sonza**.

As good Catholic girls, Annie and Eustaquia were pushed to do needlework. Instead, they lobbied to take fencing lessons, like Eustaquia's big brother. After his early demise, the sorrowing parents gave the two girls a fencing master— and a firing range of their very own at Casa de Sonza.

In the rowdy world just outside the de Sonza door, the people of Potosí were busy attending bullfights, going to fiestas, and shooting one another in duels. As youngsters, the girls had to be content with secondhand street gossip from a servant or two.

As hormones hit, however, they learned the teenage ways of sneaking out of the hacienda. From the outset, Annie and Eustaquia favored male caballero outfits—a habit that got them into various street fights. One memorable night, the teenage caballeras fought against four, whipping the cutlasses off their ruffian attackers while sustaining a number of wounds themselves. (Given the state of their clothes after these evenings, the laundress for the de Sonzas must have gotten some handsome hush money.)

Finally the great day arrived: Eustaquia came into her inheritance. By now the two young women were inseparable, and romantically intertwined. Rattling their sabers, clutching their autobiographies of **Catalina de Erauso**, a cross-dressing role model, the two set off on horseback, anxious for further adventures. The next five years wouldn't disappoint. Peru was still the Wild West of South America, and Annie and Eustaquia became part of its mystique.

Returning to Potosí, Annie decided to concentrate on *rejoneo*, the art of fighting bulls from horseback. She got very good at it. Only trouble was, the bull was better. In one painful corrida, she got gored. "Only a flesh wound!" she proclaimed. But gorings have a nasty habit of getting infected; Annie's did, and after a long illness, she died. A few months later, her bereft lover quit this earth too.

After Eustaquia and Annie made herstory, a prolific writer named Bartolomé Arzans made hay. Turned on by a portrait of the two female warriors, whom he thought "handsome and erotic," in 1736 he wrote a history of Potosí that profiled the astonishing pair. His account, which weighed in at a million words or so, is still being used as a doorstop in remote corners of Peru.

Tale of Two Bookworms

W ell-known publisher of newspapers in two states. First postmaster of Baltimore. Printer of the first signed copy of the Declaration of Independence. It sounds like Ben Franklin, but this go-getter was a lifelong single woman named **Mary Katherine Goddard**. What's more, Mary's formidable mother, **Sarah Updike Goddard**, printed and published, too.

Mom and daughter came from families that had settled Rhode Island and Long Island. Despite the handicap of an unusually good education, including studies in Latin and French, 35-year-old Sarah married a doctor. Eventually, finding herself widowed but well cushioned, she loaned half her inheritance to her son William to start a printing press and newspaper in Providence. Billy, however, could never win sufficient subscribers. In 1765 he abandoned ship and machinery, whereupon his mom and his sister Mary Katherine sprang into action. While Mary took over production, Sarah turned the *Providence Gazette* into a moneymaker, later

This is so much easier than giving Billy money!

selling it on the upswing. Bibliophile Sarah also ran a bookshop, adding luster to her reputation by doing custom bookbinding and select publishing projects. She brought out the first U.S. edition of *The Letters of Lady Mary Montagu*, the literate humanitarian who had introduced the first effective method of smallpox inoculation to Europe and the American colonies.

Wouldn't you know it, Billy popped up again, needing another fiscal transfusion; this time, he yearned to start the *Pennsylvania Chronicle*. Sarah put in capital, along with untold hours, managing the business until she was 70. Finally, she got off the hook—by dying.

Meanwhile, Mary Katherine had become a talented printer, editor, and type compositor. She took over another of Billy's startups—the *Baltimore Journal*. Even during the paper-scarce days of the Revolutionary War, she got the *Journal* out, often scooping her competitors.

What's more, in 1777 she won the honor of publishing the first true copies of the Declaration of Independence, signed by all the signatories. As an encore, she paid couriers to deliver it throughout the 13 colonies! In between printing newspapers, publishing a few almanacs, and running the bookshop, Goddard also became Baltimore's first postmaster.

At times, Mary paid postal workers herself, in coin. That hurt. Others in business, including the fledgling government, often paid workers in easily devalued paper currency or barter goods. After 14 years at the helm, however, Mary lost her job. Cutbacks? Quite the opposite. Her job had now become a federal post with a travel expense account—causing bureaucrats to label it too difficult for a woman.

Instead of wallowing in murderous fantasies, Mary Katherine retired to run her bookstore, and lived to be a sane and hearty 78.

Females Forging Ahead

Boston women have always had a stop-at-nothing attitude. Perhaps they got it from the likes of **Mary Salmon**, who inherited her late husband's forge and bellows in 1754. Soon she began running ads in the *Boston Evening Post*, assuring the horseshoe-hungry clientele that all was well: "Mary Salmon continues to carry on the business of horse-shoeing, as heretofore, where all gentlemen may have their Horses shod in the best Manner, as also all sorts of Blacksmith's Work done with Fidelity and Dispatch." Did Mary put the metal to the oatburners herself? Possibly, but not likely, given the other ads she ran for her boardinghouse, promising "to entertain boarders in a genteel manner." Since her late husband was rumored to have been poisoned, dining at Mary Salmon's, and the risks attendant, might have been part of the entertainment.

Another largely unsung Bostonian who liked a challenge was **Elizabeth Hager,** known as Handy Betty the Blacksmith for her skill with red-hot metals. Handy Betty did more than reshoe horses. During the Revolutionary War years, her ability to repair broken guns and muskets, to say nothing of the odd cannon captured from the Redcoats, made her invaluable.

During the 1700s, you could find female blacksmiths in many of the colonies. Often they were women like **Jane Burgess** of Maryland, who'd pitched in to help her husband while he was alive, and found herself the sole smith after his death in 1773. Was there consumer resistance to females doing such undainty labor? Heck no. In fact, the shortage of labor in this pre-industrial period meant that blacksmiths and other workers, whatever their gender, usually got equal pay.

Speaking of horses, what am I gonna fix for dinner?

How Nanny Got the Brits' Goat

hanghaied, kicking and screaming, from an African tribe called the Aka and taken on a slave ship to Jamaica, **Grandy Nanny** was not your average slave. Or your average woman, either, as the ruling English painfully found out.

An *obeah*, or priestess in secret African practices, she was an adept in magic and herbs. Grandy Nanny also consulted privately on matters from creating love potions to poisoning that certain obnoxious someone. She led group dances and ecstatic ceremonies of *obeah* worship that made her powerful spiritually and politically.

As she grew older, she became a leader of the Windward Maroons, one of several large groups of runaway slaves that inhabited the lush, mountainous interior of Jamaica. Before and after Nanny's day, thousands of Maroons formed independent "nations" on the island and other places around the Caribbean, and were perennial thorns in the sides of would-be white colonizers.

In 1739, Nanny and others fired up the Windward Maroons to attack the whites. (The Leeward Maroons had just signed a peace treaty, after 13 years of fighting.) For a while, the Redcoats

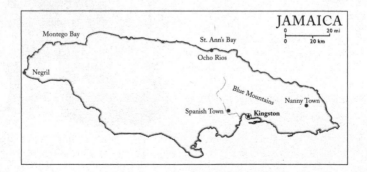

didn't get it: How could an old sorcerer woman possibly be the rebels' leader?

When the British army began a personal Nanny-hunt, she set up her headquarters in the highest reaches of the Blue Mountains. The wilderness lent itself well to guerrilla activity. With her war chief, Nanny rallied her machete-armed troops, fomented riots among locals, and fought the "red ants," as she called them, until they finally tired of the whole bloody show and signed a peace accord.

Maroons continued to live in their free societies, and ably defend them, until the end of the 18th century. Even now, inhabitants of places like Moore Town and Nanny Town proudly claim to be descendants of Grandy Nanny, one of Jamaica's six national heroes. Since 1993, archaeological teams have been excavating Nanny Town, named for the never-say-quit warrior sorceress.

Cashable Art and Other Crimes

rom an innkeeper's family, **Mary Peck Butterworth** lived at the Sign of the Black Horse in Rehoboth, a pokey village between the Massachusetts and Rhode Island colonies. Saddled with a contractor mate and a spate of seven young 'uns, she was doomed, it seemed, to the ho-hum of housewifedom.

But La Butterworth was an artiste. Secretly, she began experimenting with inks, quill pens, and fabrics. One night, it all came together: She created her own money. To be more precise, Mary made copies of the paper currencies from three colonies that were small masterpieces.

Then her *true* genius surfaced. She invented the first disposable plate for counterfeiting, fashioned from the stiff muslin of her own petticoats! It was brilliantly simple: She wet a piece of muslin, ironed it over a bill, and the image appeared on the cloth. After transferring the image to a piece of paper, she cut it to size—and threw the incriminating muslin into the fire. This was no mass-production Warhol operation, however; to make the bogus bills passable, Mary spent hours tracing each line with a quill pen.

Her business acumen matched her artistry. To distribute her growing cache of funny money, the kitchen entrepreneur enlisted her three brothers, several neighbors, a deputy sheriff, *and* people on a signup list from her own church, the Congregational Meetinghouse. Before long, Mary had to train another forger, and found a neat-handed apprentice in her sister-in-law, Hannah Peck.

Mrs. B's counterfeiting ring ran silky-smooth for seven years, and her bucks passed as legal tender in places high and low around New England. But then a careless confederate passed a Butterworth when he shouldn't have—and a keen-eyed innkeeper called the cops.

One August day in 1723, sheriffs with warrants hauled Mary Butterworth and some of her accomplices away to a jail in Bristol, Rhode Island. Their exclamations of "We broke the case!" were premature, however. The police couldn't get—and never got—any physical evidence of the ringleader's criminal activities.

Butterworth and her brother Israel went free. Frustrated, the local gendarmes kept her under surveillance for years, but the demure inventor (to their knowledge) never picked up pen or muslin again.

Funny—I used to hate ironing....

Nicotine Paydays

uring the 1600s and 1700s in the American colonies of Virginia, Georgia, Maryland, and North Carolina, enterprising women found jobs aplenty. Some occupations weren't traditionally feminine, and at times the pay stank—but not in the way you'd think.

The New World had an abundance of rivers and a scarcity of bridges; the ferryboat business boomed. Female innkeepers and planters often took on the job of maintaining ferry service across nearby rivers, and full-time posts could also be had. In Bristol Parish, Virginia, **Elizabeth Kennon** logged 15 years as a ferry mistress. Her annual salary amounted to 2,500 pounds—of *tobacco*, not British sterling.

A Maryland woman named **Elizabeth Skinner** held a similar post. The requirements for the job, administered by the court in Talbot County, said, "She would keep a good boat fit for such use and transport the inhabitants of the county, their horses and carriages, over Oxford ferry . . . as often as they shall have occasion." The county also set the ferry tolls

Not a cough in a ferryload.

Skinner would receive; in addition, they paid her 4,900 pounds of the noxious weed per year.

Even nicotine-abhorring church folks got paid in wagonloads of tobacco. As sexton of Virginia's Jones Hole Church, **Susanna Woodlief** drew 400 pounds a year. Down the road at the less affluent Sappony Church, **Sarah Williams** received a modest 250 pounds per annum of Virginia's best blond.

Currency being scarce, wages in kind were a pesky aspect of early American life. The alternatives ranged from cowhides to fresh fish. (Talk about awkward—you try making change for a mackerel.) Despite storage drawbacks, dried tobacco leaves were a much-used medium of exchange, even for physicians' fees. **Dr. Kathy Hebden** of Maryland, who whacked off limbs and administered nasty nostrums with the best of them (she wasn't the only female sawbones, either), was often paid in smoke.

Getting paid was always a problem, and Hebden had to sue for payment as often as she sutured. In desperation, she dragged her carpenter husband, Tom, into the collection side of her business. During the 1640s they became familiar faces at the provincial court. Dr. Kathy won a string of court victories, including a successful suit against George Manners and a whopping big settlement for doctoring Richard Lawrence. She even won her case against that deadbeat Edward Hall. She'd done his leg surgery but only received 10 percent of her agreed-upon fee. When the legal fur quit flying, Dr. Hebden had received all the compensation due her. What she actually collected, of course, was a small mountain of nicotine. We might call that a toxic payday, but 350 years ago tobacco was a profitable cash crop and looked on as a more benign substance than it is now.

A Fertile Brain for Scheming

 ngenious and generous—that was **Eliza Lucas Pinckney**. It didn't hurt, either, that she was born into an affluent British colonel's family. Eliza got a jolly good education, from French to Shakespeare. Like other army brats, by her teens she'd lived in Europe, the Caribbean, and North America.

In 1738, when her father inherited three rice plantations in the Carolina Colony, the Lucas family settled there. Shortly thereafter, Dad got called away to join England's new war with Spain. Instead of hiring a manager, he handed CEO duties over to his teenage daughter—the shrewdest move he ever made.

Up every morning at five, Eliza wasn't content with time-honored ways. She innovated. A pioneer in silkworm culture, she impressed the heck out of distant royalty when she had her own silk woven into a fab gift for them.

This self-taught botanist had a thing for living things—and we don't mean boyfriends. A free-spirited speller, she once wrote, "I love the vegitable world extremely." Eliza experimented with the notoriously fussy indigo plant (source of the best blue dye of the day) and got it to flourish on local soil. In 1744, this green thumb raised indigo for seed only—then gave it, and her cultivation secrets, to any planter who would grow it. The colony soon shipped more than 100,000 pounds of indigo to England, winning praise for Eliza, and a tasty tax break for her and the other colonists.

Running plantations, coping with her sickly mom, and playing the flute when she had a free moment, Eliza evaded marriage for years. Daddy sent two write-in candidates,

Eliza pioneered indigo planting and silkworm production.

adroitly rejected by Eliza. She remained a miss until age 22, when love persuaded her to wed 45-year-old widower Charles Pinckney.

An eventual three-time mom, Eliza kept her fertile brain a-boil, studying law and other such frivolous pastimes. After her husband expired of malaria, new widow Pinckney became a hands-on planter again. Now with even more plantations to run, Eliza spent the next 40 years zestfully carrying out her best ideas, from growing figs for export to teaching her slave girls to read and write. When Eliza died of cancer on May 26, 1793,

George Washington was among those who asked to be a pallbearer for the woman who had honored her "own true self," as she put it.

It's pleasant to find that Eliza's traits duly survived in her only daughter, **Harriott Horry**, who also married late, got widowed early, stayed single, ran a plantation, and savored life to the fullest.

Our first prez was proud to be Eliza's pallbearer.

What "Love Slave" Once Meant

Two hundred years after her carnal capers with a U.S. president, **Sally Hemings** has finally gotten satisfaction. Her long-term relationship with Thomas Jefferson, human rights booster and lifelong slaveholder, has been borne out by DNA testing of their descendants.

Born a slave in 1773, young Sally came to Monticello plantation in Virginia the year after Tom Jefferson married **Martha Wayles**. Although they weren't gift-wrapped, Sally and her mother, Betty, were wedding presents from the Wayleses. In sordid fact, Sally and several of her siblings had the same randy, equal-opportunity white father as Tom's new bride. That made Martha and Sally half-sisters—no wonder both women proved irresistible to Tom.

When Dashing Sally was in her early teens, she consoled lonely guy Jefferson, who by then was moping, wifeless at 45, around the plantation. When Tom won the post of ambassador to France, he asked Sally to bring over his younger daughter,

Slave cabin, Sally's home.

Polly. Besides getting to see the sights and suck up a few escargots, Sally lapped up some education—and the eye-opening notion of being a free woman, at least while in France.

Three years later, when Jefferson and Hemings returned to Virginia in 1789, they were an item. Soon Sally popped out a son, and then another, and so on, for a total of five or six children, some or all of them fathered by Thomas J., it's now believed.

Although he and Sally had a long-term intimacy, Jefferson was oh-so-conflicted about miscegenation—to say nothing of slavery itself. Here was a guy with vast landholdings, huge indebtedness (thanks to his incessant rebuilding of Monticello), and 200 slaves. He didn't hold with the mixing of the races, yet that was how he lived his life. He became famous for his writings on freedom; but in later life he advocated diffusion, the quaint notion that allowing slavery to spread beyond the South was the best way to end it!

When tall, red-haired, light-eyed Jefferson died in 1826, there were dozens of tall, ruddy, light-complected slaves to mourn him. In life he had agonized over keeping his "slave family" intact. Nevertheless,

Monticello mansion, Jefferson's home.

Jefferson's debts were such that 130 humans were sold down the river after his funeral—including a couple of the Hemings clan. As if that weren't low enough of a blow, Sally didn't even get freed in Tom's will. She was eventually manumitted by one of Jefferson's white daughters. Surrounded by her descendants, the dashing one lived into her 60s.

The Molly Pitcher Heroines

ike the term "G.I. Joe," "Molly Pitcher" became a generic nickname, earned by the gutsiest Revolutionary War gals to see military action. These women of humble backgrounds did much more than haul pitchers of H_2O to cool cannon barrels and parched troops, however.

The earliest documented "pitcher" on the mound was **Margaret Corbin**. During the Battle of Fort Washington in Manhattan in 1776, this 25-year-old aided her husband, John, a private in the Pennsylvania artillery corps. As the Hessian soldiers blasted away at them, Margaret swabbed out the Big Bertha between firings (a tidy cannon is a functioning cannon, she'd been told), helping John ram in the next ball. At length, the enemy scored a fatal slam-dunk on her husband. Margaret immediately took over his fieldpiece until she, too, was riddled by hostile fire.

Three years after that November battle, with one arm permanently useless and now assigned to the Invalid Regiment at West Point, Margaret was awarded the first military pension ever given to a woman. (Other female vets would wait up to 40 years to receive theirs.) Corbin's award? Disability pay for life (at half the going rate for disabled males), a set of clothes, and a monthly liquor ration. Overwhelmed by their generosity,

Margaret didn't start squawking until it became clear that she couldn't collect any liquid refreshment, since issuing booze to women was forbidden. In 1782, she finally submitted a bill for the 257 gills of whiskey due her. Only after further delays did a disgruntled Corbin receive her cache of bottles.

The toughest challenge Corbin faced, however, was living on her miserable pension—although military folks who knew her tried to help out. Wearing her raunchy old Army coat, Margaret had to augment her diet by fishing off the docks. By then she was a slightly batty old vet of 50, who insisted on being saluted as "Captain Molly." A century after her death, she was reburied with honors by the D.A.R. at West Point cemetery.

Another Molly Pitcher whose deeds were long repeated was Pennsylvanian **Mary Ludwig Hays McCauley**, a tobacco-chewing trooper who saw action at the Battle of Monmouth, New Jersey. On that long hot June day in 1778, Mary helped her husband, William, load the cannon.

How do you expect a cannon operator to work with a corpse underfoot?

When he took a bullet, she jumped in. This 20-something had nerve. An amazed eyewitness saw a British cannonball pass between her legs, ripping away the bottom half of her garments. Mary gamely returned fire, saying, "Lucky for me the thing didn't carry off something I really valued!"

After the war, and two husbands later, Mary finally received a $40 annual pension in 1822. From then on, she lived at the Carlisle post, cooking for the soldiers and reliving battles with anyone who would listen.

Light Spying and Graver Matters

 tiny Irishwoman, intelligent, flexible, and full of fight, **Lydia Darragh** landed in Philadelphia with her growing family in the mid-1700s. Lydia loved to doctor people. A midwife of note, she had lots of hands-on practice and herbal common sense as well.

However, she may have done more business at the other end of the life/death continuum, judging by her 1766 ad in the *Pennsylvania Gazette:* "Lydia Darragh, living in Second Street, at the corner of Taylor's Alley, opposite the Golden Fleece Tavern, takes this method of informing the Public that she intends to make Grave-Clothes, and lay out the Dead, in the Neatest Manner."

A Quaker like her husband, William, Lydia quietly carried off major heroics during the Revolutionary War. When the British occupied the city, they commandeered a room in the Darragh house to hold strategy meetings. Lydia and company weren't asked to vacate—just go up to bed, and stay there, were the orders. (The Brits assumed that, being Quaker pacifists, the Darraghs would be neutral.)

At first, spying was a family affair: When Lydia got a juicy bit of news, her husband wrote it in shorthand. She then hid it inside one or more big buttons, sewed them on her younger son's jacket, and had him deliver the data to her older son, serving in the Army at Washington's camp.

On the night of December 2, 1777, the British held a super-secret skull session. Lydia listened at the door and heard a bombshell: British troops were going to attack the Americans at Whitemarsh in three days! Mild-mannered Lydia devised a daring plan. First she wangled a pass to go through British lines, saying that the family needed flour. After walking five miles to the mill, she found a Yankee scout, passed on her information (hidden in a piece of needlework), grabbed her flour, and booked it for home.

Shortly thereafter, the Redcoats took a royal whipping at that battle—and a suspicious officer came to interrogate Lydia. Luckily, like many a prosecuting attorney, he asked her the wrong questions, so she didn't have to lie. This great-hearted patriot in a small package lived until 1789. (But not as a Quaker—the local Society of Friends expelled the Darraghs and their older son for being altogether too martial.) When she died, the town responded with a fulsome obituary, a well-attended funeral, and—one hopes—someone to lay her out "in the neatest manner," as Lydia Darragh herself would have done.

A Quaker mom who stuck her neck out.

Bolívar's Secret Weapon

"Gentle, crazy woman" was merely one of the admiring remarks directed at **Manuela Sáenz**, this one from her lover, continent liberator Simón Bolívar.

Ecuadorian Manuela had that kind of checkered past so beloved in soap operas: She was illegitimate, did time in a nunnery, had a runaway love affair, and was pushed into marriage with a dull English doctor.

By 1819, the countries of Ecuador, Bolivia, Peru, Colombia, and Venezuela were hip-deep in revolution. Refusing to stick to matters marital, Manuela offered her skills—good brain, sharp tongue, guts, sex appeal—to the movement. At a liberation parade in 1822, she got a look at Bolívar, the man of the year, a tubercular-thin, big-nosed guy with a long sad face. When he looked up, she threw him a laurel wreath. That night, they danced and romanced at the victory ball—the beginning of an eight-year passion.

Chucking what few social conventions she honored, Manuela flaunted their relationship; frequently apart, the couple wrote voluminously, although she never had Simón's undivided attention. It's a wonder he got any battles won, given the stream of ladies he entertained.

Bolívar had a disturbing attitude toward women:

I used to be a continent liberator, y'know.

He dug their support, loved their money, and cherished their organizing abilities, especially Manuela's. But when it came to women enjoying full rights of citizenship in the new republics, he was against it.

Love-myopic Manuela continued to carry out spy operations and accompany Bolívar's armies into battle. Before long, however, Latino politics turned against Bolívar.

Manuela's life became a nightmare. She intercepted a series of death plots and saved Simón's life at a masquerade ball. In 1825, she foiled more conspirators, who sword-whipped her so stingingly that she spent two weeks in bed. All her loyalty and help couldn't turn the political tide—or save Bolívar's life. He died of tuberculosis (and defeat) in 1830.

At length, Manuela Sáenz was driven from Colombia and exiled to Jamaica. Eventually she opened a tobacco shop on the

Peru-Ecuador border, where she grew old and plump, still feisty and full of tales of herself and the Liberator, whom she outlived by 26 years. At length, Ecuador and the rest of South America paid her homage—the most beautiful gesture being a poem by Nobel laureate Pablo Neruda.

Bum Start, Photo Finish

 aving a weakness for joy-riding on someone else's horse could mean very bad news in 18th-century England, as **Mary Haydock Reibey** certainly knew. Thirteen years old, a runaway, and dressed as a boy, she was caught trying to peddle a hot nag and was given a death sentence. Then the judge relented, merely shipping Mary off to Australia for seven years of hard labor.

In October 1792, Mary landed in New South Wales. Thanks to her literacy and educated speech, she got one of the few legitimate jobs available: She became a nursemaid and housekeeper to the lieutenant governor's family.

There she met Tom Reibey, first mate for the East India Company. Despite her criminal status, sparks flew. In 1794, Mary and the young Irishman were given permission to wed.

There was no honeymoon, but upon marriage those seven years of servitude just vanished. The couple homesteaded a farm, started a cargo and trading business, and began a family that

*True fame:
When you're in the money—
and on it.*

came to number seven kids. Mary kept the accounts and ran their store.

Reibey, always more at ease at sea than on land, began to make trading trips. On one of his voyages to India, he came home with a fever and died in 1811. A month later, his business partner keeled over. At age 34, Mary had to take charge of their business, which boasted three ships, a warehouse, several farms, a hotel, and trading clients in China, India, and elsewhere.

From Entally House, her stone mansion in Sydney, she added to her shipping line—and her bottom line—with new warehouses, vessels, and real estate. In nine years, she possessed a fortune of 20,000 pounds! Not too shabby for an ex-con.

It was time for some personal pampering, she declared, taking two of her daughters to England—but she'd forgotten how cold, damp, and socially cramped the place was.

In 1821 she returned to her Aussie home, a move she hoped would erase her first, fettered arrival as a teenage convict. Deciding that she kinda liked being single, Mary remained that way. At age 51, she retired to continue her good works. Besides giving to charities, she took an active role in education as one of the governors of the Free Grammar School.

Even at this stage, Aussie society remained cruelly snobbish. To the end of her life, Mary wore the "convict taint." Nevertheless, she forged ahead, and saw that her children married well—to society snobs, of course.

In a final triumph over her humble beginnings, Mary Haydock Reibey was honored by her adoptive country in a special way: Her droll and spectacled likeness appears on the Australian $20 bill—a photo finish for a mighty dark horse.

Female Mutiny, after the Bounty

It was no luau, making a home on Pitcairn Island. **Jenny Teehuteaunua** was used to Tahiti; her *Bounty* mutineer "husbands" were no prizes either. Alone among the 11 women on Pitcairn, Jenny had no children. In 1794, after enduring years of spousal abuse, and mayhem that shrank the male population, she said to the other gals, "Let's leave the island!" That attempt failed; undeterred, Jenny and company conspired to wipe out the remaining whites while they slept. The mass-murder plot bombed too. However, Tahitian grrl power did make the men very, very nervous. After that, whenever Jenny or any of the other women got fed up, they snatched up the kids and the firearms, and hid out in a remote area.

In 1817, the whaler ship *Sultan* stopped at Pitcairn. Without a backward glance, Jenny was aboard when it sailed. Her eyewitness account of the mutiny and the bloody happenings on Pitcairn was taken down and published in an 1819 issue of Australia's *Sydney Gazette* and later in the *United Service Journal*. Fascinating reading, it's now available online as well. What's more, her tale has been confirmed by archaeology on Pitcairn.

Okay, who thought running away from paradise was a good idea?

Dream Weaver

igh human drama can be found on a scrap of paper. Take the single extant letter written by **Hannah Harris**, a Virginia slave on plantation Leo, one of 18 belonging to slaveholder-planter Robert Carter. Besides being literate, Hannah was a talented weaver. Her owner even rented out her flax-weaving skills.

For a man who held thousands of human beings as chattel, Carter wasn't a bad guy. Prodded by the enlightened laws passed by Virginia in 1782 after the Revolutionary War, or by conscience and his religious conversion from Baptist to the Swedenborgian America New Church, he began proceedings to free his slaves. Not all at once, you understand—that would be inconvenient. This was a timed release of 500 slaves over 21 years.

When 1792 rolled around, Hannah got the news. "Congrats! You'll be freed next January," her owner said. Thirty-seven-year-old Hannah sat down and wrote him a letter. A mushy "Thank you, master" note, perhaps? Not a chance. Like others in human bondage, Hannah thought hard about her future. She asked Carter if she could buy back her own loom— to make a living once free. Was her request granted? Most probably. In the relatively tolerant years between 1782 and 1800, more than 10,000 slaves like Hannah Harris were freed in Virginia.

A Widow's Bubbly New World

 sually it was the wife who died after childbirth. In the case of Frenchwoman **Nicole-Barbe Clicquot,** she and her baby girl survived, and her husband *c'était fini.* Married just three years, the 20-year-old donned mourning clothes and adopted the funereal handle of La Veuve Clicquot (the widow of Clicquot).

Daughter of the mayor of Reims, Nicole had gotten interested in vineyards and the making of champagne when she wed her short-lived winemaker in 1799. Now, under her own steam, she started hands-on experimentation. At that time, the addition of sugar and yeast to make champagne produced a beverage that was sludgy rather than scintillating. One day, Nicole had an ingenious idea: Why not store the bottles upside-down while they aged, to see if the sludge would work its way into the neck? She fooled around with giving the bottles a quarter-turn over the months. After a lot of messy experimentation (you shoulda seen that winery floor) she pioneered a way to whip out the cork, expel the sediment, and recork without losing the liquid.

After tasting her new clear-as-a-bell champagne, the young widow cried, *"Formidable—vive la Veuve!"* while her competitors slapped their foreheads in why-didn't-I think-of-that gestures, and gloomily drank all her samples.

By 1814, the tedious wars that France had been fighting—first with the British and then with their own Napoleon—came to an end. Clicquot's business shot ahead like a well-aimed champagne cork, leaving her more sedimentary competitors a distant second, third, fourth. (One of her better customers was former Empress Josephine, who ran up such a tab that it became a hot-button item in her divorce from Bonaparte.)

Not one to sit on her laurels, Nicole triumphed again with her pink champagne innovation. At age 43, Madame was able to retire to her château de Boursault in Boursin, living to a hearty 89 and still getting her daily exercise from lifting a glass of bubbly.

Perhaps even more than their French counterparts, women in America appreciated Nicole's breakthrough. At that time, the United States was awash in rum, beer, gin, whiskey, and other nongenteel drinks—not a romantic bubble in the bunch.

When Clicquot came up with her winning way of making see-through champagne, she soon won a devoted new following across the Atlantic.

Revered by Far Too Few

Two years after Paul Revere's much-swooned-over midnight ride, a 16-year-old from Fredericksburg, New York, rode her favorite horse, Star, to warn of another British approach. On *her* rain-soaked ride of April 26, 1777, **Sybil Ludington** galloped twice as far as Paul Revere, knocking on farmhouse doors along a 40-mile route. "Two thousand Redcoats are raiding Danbury—muster at Ludington's!" was her message. Sybil must have been quite a horsewoman; her route was rugged, hilly, and fraught with danger. At one point the young woman had to ward off a highwayman with her dad's musket. Although she roused a substantial number of volunteers, enemy troops managed to escape to their ships. Sybil's hometown was later renamed Ludingtonville in her honor.

There were revered deeds by other heroines on horseback, too, including 22-year-old **Deborah Champion**, who rode from her home in Connecticut for two days to reach George Washington with urgent dispatches from her region. She bluffed her way through enemy lines, later writing about her mission: "Pulling my calash cap still further over my face, I went on with what boldness I could muster. Suddenly I was ordered to halt. . . . A soldier in a red coat proceeded to take me to headquarters, but I told him it was too early to wake the captain and to please let me pass for I had been sent in urgent haste to see a friend in need, which was true if ambiguous. To my joy, he let me go, saying, 'Well, you are only an old woman anyway,' evidently as glad to get rid of me as I of him."

Unlike icon Paul Revere, who was captured by the Brits ten miles into his ride (Longfellow's poem failed to mention that little mishap), Sybil and Deborah both completed their missions.

Too bad Sybil's 1975 commemorative stamp doesn't say what she did!

A Bargain Flag and a Fairy Tale

altimore widow **Mary Young Pickersgill**, needle-woman extraordinaire, often worked with her mother on sewing jobs large and small. The commission that came through Mary's door in 1813, however, was a doozy. America was at war with the British—again. As the commander of nearby Fort McHenry explained, "We want one standard-sized flag, *plus* a really big sucker that those bloody Brits can see from a distance."

A true patriot, Mary didn't even demand a deposit but set to work on a banner 42 feet long and 30 feet wide. This monster used 400 yards of wool, weighed 85 pounds, and had to be assembled on the floor of a brewery, by candlelight. Besides mom, Mary enlisted other pro seamstresses. They made more than 1.7 million stitches to complete the flag.

In September 1814, the British launched a savage attack on the fort. A lawyer named Francis Scott Key happened to be on a ship in the river, and watched the lengthy battle. When dawn came and the smoke cleared, he saw Mary's flag, flying defiantly high. It was a real goose-bump moment, inspiring him to compose the "Star-Spangled Banner" then and there. His lyrics became our national anthem—and Mary's flag became known as Old Glory.

Newly refurbished, this superb artifact holds a place of honor at the Smithsonian Institution in Washington, D.C. In Baltimore there's an equally fascinating primary source document from Pickersgill's life: her handwritten invoice for the job. Unlike the average Pentagon purchase of today, Old Glory cost the taxpayers a modest $405.90.

The true biography of **Betsy Ross**, another widow, who

Cheer up gals—only 20 feet to go!

lived in earlier Revolutionary times, has ironic parallels. Born a Quaker, Betsy got drummed out of her church when she wed Anglican upholsterer John Ross. Two years later, John died in a gunpowder explosion, but at least Betsy had learned a trade that complemented her sewing skills. Betsy was widowed twice more; she had five daughters with husband number three before he was paralyzed and perished in 1817.

Betsy valiantly carried on as parent and breadwinner for decades, supporting her family by sewing. In 1777, she may have whipped up several flags for the navy, but there is no evidence that she made the first U.S. flag at George Washington's behest, or anyone else's. There were no shopping trips to her upholstery shop by a congressional committee, either.

After Betsy's death, the whole warm and fuzzy story was concocted in 1876 by her grandson Bill Canby as the nation's centennial approached. In a speech, Bill asserted that his granny had made the first flag with her own hands. Even then, most people didn't buy it. But the young nation was about to celebrate its 100th birthday, and needed some heartwarming history—fast. A Betsy Ross memorial association soon sprang up, selling two million memberships at a dime each. Other validation, including canvases painted by Charles Weisberger, lent credence to the Betsy first flag myth. The fairy tale took flight, finding its way like a computer virus into books and periodicals. Betsy Ross was extraordinary, but not in the way she has been labeled. Unsung Mary was even more extraordinary—and has finally received her just due.

Mom-and-daughter Voodoo

For three-quarters of a century, an artful woman named **Marie Laveau** was one of the hottest tickets in New Orleans. A superb cook and a hairdresser, the art for which she became famous locally had a darker hue. Marie was a voodoo queen.

Born free in 1794 in the French colony then called Saint-Dominique (part of Haiti today), Marie fled to New Orleans after that island's bloody slave uprising. A café au lait beauty, she married another refugee, a free black named Jacques Paris. Together they had some 15 children, including her lookalike daughter Marie.

With all those mouths to feed, Marie took her culinary and coiffure skills to a place with a huge captive audience: the New Orleans city jail. Granted, the tips weren't all that great. And the ambiance? Fuhgeddaboutit. No *bons temps* rolling at all.

But Marie schmoozed as she cooked and combed, filing away off-the-record confidences and dirty linen details on locals from white politicos to black debutantes, learning whose skeletons were in what closet, and so on. That data bank became her key to business success when Marie started her own voodoo hotline. (First, however, she took night classes with early New Orleans legend Dr. John, whose excellent spy system she emulated.)

For decades, people came to high priestess Laveau seeking

love charms, clairvoyant readings about future enterprises, and treatment of physical ailments. Celebrities, society women, ambitious politicians all knocked on her door on St. Ann Street. Marie didn't ignore ordinary folks, either. Even slaves showed up, seeking secret guidance for escape attempts! (Poor clients got dinged ten bucks per visit, while the sliding scale went up-up-up for the well-heeled.)

At that time, there were more than 300 voodoo practitioners in the city, but only Marie was called the Boss Woman. On Bayou St. John she held standing-room-only rituals, the most famous of which took place on June 24 each year. Her show-stopping program included beheading live roosters and dirty dancing with Zombi, her ten-foot-long snake.

In later years, Marie got a little bored with pure voodoo and started sticking Catholic touches, from holy water to incense, into her shtick. By the time she took up residence in her fetish-decorated tomb in 1881, the *New Orleans Picayune* newspaper eulogized, "All in all, Marie Laveau was a wonderful woman. She died with a firm trust in heaven."

As canny as her mother, daughter **Marie Laveau** took up data mining and voodoodom where La Laveau left off, and accumulated equal power and wealth.

The Big Bang

Brave new world, *c'est moi*, said **Marie-Madeleine-Sophie Armant Blanchard**, as she and a hot-air balloon headed skyward around 1800. Second wife of crotchety French balloonist Jean-Pierre Blanchard, who'd already flown many strange beasts of the air, Marie felt it was high time she got high. When she and the recent widower had met at his ascent in 1798, *l'amour* had struck. Eighteen-year-old Marie-Madeleine was dazzled by Jean-Pierre. Her new mate had flopped in his recent try at conquering America by air, but with her at his side, they would conquer the world by basket.

But I wanted to go zat way!

On Marie's maiden flight, France was at her feet. Literally. This ballooning thing was fabulous. The only thing that got her petticoats in a twist was the thought of that hussy, **Marie Elizabeth Thible**, the French opera diva who'd had the honor of being the first woman aloft on a free flight. People were still gasping over the way she'd flown high over Lyons for 45 minutes on June 4, 1784.

Still, the new Mrs. Blanchard was giving the lighter-than-air industry a little glamour. Her costumes! Her themed ascents! *Très magnifique!* Pretty soon La Blanchard had clocked more than 40 events. She got terrific press from her 1810 Wedding Special ascent for the nuptials of Napoleon and Marie-Louise of

Austria. The royals ate it up—everyone except Josephine, who was still vexed over Bonaparte's annulment of their marriage.

Marie's sole problem: how to top her successes. In 1819, a buxom 39 and still looking good, Marie-Madeleine planned a pièce de résistance. Forget hot-air balloons—she was ready for some serious aeronautics: a hydrogen balloon ascent, framed by a thrilling fireworks display. On July 6, the balloon—and Marie—went up.

Jean-Pierre wasn't there to see it, having unluckily taken the fast lane in a parachute descent ten years earlier. Still, he would have tingled at the magnitude of Marie's show. Gorgeously costumed and waving the flag of France, she ascended to the heavens in a cockleshell like that of Botticelli's *Venus*.

At the peak of the action, however, the fireworks acted as a fuse for her flammable vehicle, setting off the most memorable fire and explosion France (and neighboring countries) had ever seen. Intrepid Marie became airborne in a way she hadn't planned on—and ballooning suffered its first female casualty.

Although it was fatal, Madame B's feat only fanned the flames of ballooning frenzy across the Atlantic. A mere six years later, the world would goggle at the first female Yank to soar solo.

High-flying Vixens

 n the balloon-happy United States, aerostation-worshipping women were as suicidally daring as their European counterparts. Inspired by the kamikaze feats of France's Marie Blanchard, on October 24, 1825, a mysterious **Madam Johnson** made a solo flight from Castle Garden, a pleasure park in New York City. The "fair voyager," as she was dubbed by newspaper reporters, landed in a Long Island salt marsh. After her maiden voyage, Johnson enjoyed three years of successful gas balloon launches in New Jersey, New York, and Pennsylvania. The biggest hang-up with ballooning in Johnson's day? The high cost of inflating the envelope with hydrogen gas. Would-be flyers had to have fat checkbooks—or do pay-per-view. Johnson had a firm policy. If she didn't take in enough at the gate, she wouldn't go up. Her resolve set off several near-riots in Philadelphia and Manhattan.

Always a hotbed of hot air—and ballooning, too—Philadelphia boasted its own female aeronaut, the equally mysterious **Madam Delon**. On the morning of June 25, 1856, two seasoned aeronauts helped her inflate her balloon. Delon lifted off from the corner of Callowhill and Seventh streets, headed over the Delaware River, and sailed sedately over four villages before landing safely in Tacony in time for dinner. Her time aloft—supposedly more than seven hours—caused amazement back then, as it would today as well.

Pay-per-view, the only way to fly.

Heavy Irony

Brandywine Iron Works co-owner **Rebecca Pennock Lukens** had her hands full with three kids and a newborn baby, when in 1825 her loving husband did the meanest thing: He died.

Besides draping crepe, her employees wanted to know: What about the huge order the plant had received to make plate for the USS *Codorus*, the first American ironclad warship?

Full speed ahead, said Rebecca. But first she had to battle her cranky mother, her crankier bank, her husband's lack of a will, her dad's ambiguous will, and her own learning curve. Behind schedule, the company was also teetering near bankruptcy from expansion. With her brother-in-law overseeing the plant, Lukens tackled arcane matters, from squeezing out financing to purchasing raw materials. Solo, she learned to deliver orders on time—and set prices that turned a profit. After a near-speed-of-light effort, the *Codorus* order was duly delivered to York, Pennsylvania.

From that stressful beginning, Rebecca built her company into a major player in the iron plate biz. Besides commissions for seagoing vessels, she won contracts to make locomotives and Mississippi steamboats. With her at the helm, her company weathered the U.S. financial panic of 1837.

Through it all, her Quaker mom uttered the same refrain: "Thou art out of line!" It wasn't easy to ignore the old bat, since she carried the debt on Rebecca's enterprise. Lukens had other opposition—the mills downstream, for instance, whose owners leaned on her for more water. Rebecca just leaned back.

As Quakers, her Pennsylvania family held the philosophy that women had brains and potential. As a student, Rebecca had waded into higher math, French, botany, chemistry, and static electricity (not a major you see much any more). She'd tagged after her dad in the mill, seeing how sheets of iron were slitted into rods for blacksmith use. After her marriage, she got further industry insights. She'd come to agree with her husband that big iron plates—and big contracts—represented their future.

Over time, Rebecca Lukens became a woman of wealth, a leading citizen, and an enlightened employer. She built houses for her workers, awarded bonuses for reaching mill output goals, and provided working conditions that were better than most of her era. Five years after her death at 58, the company honored Rebecca by renaming itself Lukens Iron Works (later Lukens Steel Company, which it remains to this day).

A Kinder, Gentler, More Musical Sing Sing

Think of a matron at a famous federal penitentiary like Sing Sing, and you envision a crusty old gal or a Nurse Ratchet type. **Eliza Wood Farnham** was neither. At 29, this New Yorker was already a well-known social reformer when she got called to the Big House.

As women's matron, Farnham made a number of humane changes. Until her tenure, female prisoners had been allowed to work and eat together—but only in *total silence*. Talk about cruel and unusual punishment! Not surprisingly, this policy from the governing board had led to riots. As matron, Farnham brought many humanizing touches: She allowed prisoners to have books, flowers,

Sing Sing singalong.

curtains—even dolls. She also brought in a piano and encouraged singalongs and other social events.

After serving as matron for four years, a widowed Farnham moved to California, where she started a society to help women without resources migrate west.

Even after remarriage, this altruist pushed for higher education and careers for women, and wrote several worthy books, the most widely read being *Woman and Her Era*. Her *Life in Prairie Land* is still in print.

Peak Experiences of the Kapiolanis

 ne day in 1820 the top spiritual leader of Hawaii was minding her own business, getting a coconut-oil rubdown, and catching some rays at Kailua-Kona beach when a boatload of pale people showed up. The poor things were burdened with the most ungainly black garments, but they seemed to take to her. These folks were hawking a new religion called Christianity. **Kapiolani** wasn't sure about its single deity provision, but she did like the idea of one husband per customer. As high priestess, she had a wearisome number of spouses (two, possibly more) to look after.

You had to be in peak shape physically to be a Polynesian high priestess. Born in Hilo, on the Big Island, Kapiolani used real peaks to stay trim. In 1824, after accepting Christianity, she did a 60-mile barefoot hike over the sharp lava rock, and that was the easy part. She then made a sizzling descent into Kilauea crater, defying the much-feared Hawaiian goddess Pele. She challenged Pele by refusing to make the traditional offerings.

Worse yet, she munched a bunch of the sacred *'ohelo* berries that grew near the crater—a *big* taboo.

By now Kapiolani had slimmed down to one god and one husband, who was probably screaming encouragement from the sidelines. When her daring feats failed to provoke a volcanic eruption, it so impressed her followers that the signup queue for Christian baptism ran halfway down the lava flow.

The missionaries, still sickly pale and unbecomingly over-dressed, were gleeful at her showmanship. At that point, Kapiolani tried to cut a deal. "We'll accept Christianity, but I warn you—-there's no way we're going to wear those outfits of yours," she said. It's tragic to relate, but Kapiolani lost that argument. All too soon, the capacious bodies of Hawaiian royalty were squeezed into tight-fitting black garments more suitable to a New England climate. Eventually, however, Hawaiians rebelled against Victorian sartorial torture. Thus was born the garment known to millions today as the muu-muu.

Kapiolani traveled to Honolulu, where she learned to read

and write, but she lived near the south Kona coast most of her life. A gardener, she experimented with guavas, oranges, and the crop that would become a modern American addiction, Kona coffee beans.

At age 60, Kapiolani leaned on her spiritual connections when she got breast cancer, stoically enduring a radical mastectomy without a wisp of painkiller. She survived it, too—only to expire a few months later from a fever. Fittingly, there are numerous cancer centers, schools, and hospitals named for this valiant, vibrant *wahine*.

A second royal Kapiolani, born on the island of Kauai, became Hawaii's queen upon her marriage to King Kalakaua. **Queen Kapiolani** bore no children, and the couple's turbulent reign was marked by the revels of her husband, which were described by the *New York Times* as "orgies in the palace." Recoiling in disgust, the queen turned to travel and good works, journeying to England for the 1887 jubilee of Queen Victoria, and founding a home for girls afflicted with Hansen's disease (leprosy) on her home island. Like the volcano-leaping Kapiolani, the queen suffered from cancer, succumbing to it in 1899 at age 65.

BIBLIOGRAPHY

The core material for this omnibus comes from four decades of historical detective work. I delved into the works of hundreds of writers from ancient Greek, Roman, and Mesopotamian times through medieval, Renaissance, and colonial periods; scholarly tomes, PhD theses, and archaeological reports and interviews. I visited many of the countries of origin and their museum collections. I drew from a mountain of primary source materials, from papyri and coinage to artwork and artifacts, from Mediterranean lands, Asia, the New World, Australia, and elsewhere.

The most useful primary sources for women from antiquity through A.D. 400 are the **Loeb Classical Library** volumes, especially *Select Papyri* (2 volumes by Hunt and Edgar) and the volumes by Athenaeus, Cicero, Dio Cassius, Diodorus Siculus, Diogenes Laertius, Herodotus, Iamblicus, Jerome, Josephus, Martial, Pausanias, Pliny the Elder, Plutarch, Procopius, Seneca, Strabo, Suetonius, Tacitus, and Xenophon. (The Landmark editions of Herodotus and others are particularly valuable.) Other compilations containing invaluable materials include Kenneth Sylvan Guthrie's *Pythagorean Sourcebook*; Shelton's *As the Romans Did*; and Guido Majno's *The Healing Hand*.

To me, the most exciting development in historical research since I first began working on the four-book *Uppity Women* series in 1994 has been the publication of works produced by the women profiled in this volume. As of this writing, the following items by or about these women are available in new, used, and/or electronic editions. (Another recent development has been websites such as Wiki Commons that have opened up a world of public domain images, including woodcuts, engravings, paintings, and early photographs of long-ago women and their creations.)

NOTE: *Due to limited space, publishers and publication dates are not given for this section.*

Al-Adawiya, Rabi'a. *Doorkeeper of the Heart.*

Andalus Poets (includes Wallada al-Mustakfi).

Behn, Aphra Amis. *The Rover and Other Plays* (and other works).

Clare of Assisi. *Early Documents.*

Cleopatra: A Sourcebook.

Clifford, Anne. *The Diaries of Lady Anne Clifford.*

Colonna, Vittoria. *Sonnets of Michelangelo* (and other works).

Comnena, Anna. *The Alexiad.*

De Erauso, Catalina. *Lieutenant Nun.*

Farnham, Eliza Wood. *Life in Prairie Land* (and other works).

Fell, Margaret. *Undaunted Zeal: The Letters of Margaret Fell.*

Heloise. *Letters of Abelard and Heloise.*

Hildegard of Bingen. *Physica* (and other works); *Illuminations* (her artwork); various CDs of her music.

Joan of Arc. *By Herself and Her Witnesses.*

Kapiolani. *Heroine of Hawaii, or Triumph of Grace at the Sandwich Islands.*

Kempe, Margery. *The Book of Margery Kempe.*

Lukens, Rebecca. *A Woman in Steel.*

Montagu, Lady Mary Wortley. *Selected Letters* (and other works).

Murasaki, Lady. *Tale of Genji.*

Nijo, Lady. *Confessions of Lady Nijo.*

Pinckney, Eliza Lucas. *The Letterbook of Eliza Lucas Pinckney, 1739–1762.*

Reibey, Mary Haydock. *Dear Cousin: The Letters of the Reibeys.*

Rowlandson, Mary. *Captivity and Restoration of Mrs. Mary Rowlandson.*

Shipton, Mother. *Mother Shipton's Prophesies.*

Trotula. *The Trotula* (Monica Green, editor and translator).

Williams, Eunice. *The Unredeemed Captive.*

Recommended Secondary Sources

Amt, Emilie, ed. *Women's Lives in Medieval Europe: A Sourcebook* (Routledge Chapman, 1993).

Barstow, Anne L. *Witchcraze* (HarperCollins, 1994).

Berkin, Carol. *First Generations: Women in Colonial America* (Hill & Wang, 1996).

Bogin, Meg. *The Woman Troubadours* (Norton, 1980).

Borzello, Frances. *Seeing Ourselves: Self Portraits by Women Artists* (Abrams, 1988).

Brown, Judith C. *Immodest Acts: the Life of a Lesbian Nun in Renaissance Italy* (Oxford University Press, 1986).

Dekker, Rudolf, and van de Pol, Lotte. *The Tradition of Female Transvestism in Early Modern Europe* (St. Martins Press, 1989).

Feinberg, Leslie. *Transgender Warriors* (Beacon Press, 1996).

Fantham, Elaine, et al, eds. *Women in the Classical World* (Oxford University Press, 1994).

Fraser, Antonia. *The Warrior Queens* (Vintage Books, 1988).

——. *The Weaker Vessel* (Vintage Books, 1994).

Henry, Sondra, and Taitz, Emily. *Written out of History: Jewish Foremothers* (Biblio Press, 1990).

Herlihy, David. *Opera Muliebria: Women and Work in Medieval Europe* (McGraw Hill, 1990).

Hirshfield, Jane, ed. *Women in Praise of the Sacred* (HarperCollins, 1994).

Hogrefe, Pearl. *Tudor Women: Commoners & Queens* (Iowa State University Press, 1975).

Larrington, Carolyne. *Women and Writing in Medieval Europe: A Sourcebook* (Routledge, 1995).

Moynihan, Ruth, et al, eds. *Second to None: A Documentary of American Women*, Vol. 1 (University of Nebraska Press, 1993).

Norton, Mary Beth. *Founding Mothers & Fathers* (Vintage, 1997).

Snyder, Jane M. *The Woman and the Lyre* (Southern Illinois University Press, 1989).

Spruill, Julia C. *Women's Life & Work in the Southern Colonies* (Norton, 1972).

Uitz, Erika. *The Legend of Good Women* (Moyer Bell, 1994).

Wiesner, Merry. *Working Women in Renaissance Germany* (Rutgers University Press, 1986).

Williams, Selma. *Demeter's Daughters* (Atheneum, 1976).

Wittkower, Rudolf and Margot. *Born Under Saturn: The Character and Conduct of Artists* (Random House, 1963).

Online Resources for Long-ago Women

- http://www.livius.org. A comprehensive, well-organized, easily searchable website on antiquity.

- http://penelope.uchicago.edu/Thayer. Portal to the vast Lacus Curtius website, crammed with ancient lore and translations, with wonderful commentary.

- http://passionateabouthistory.blogspot.com. The impressive online works of Mary Harrsch, including her blog History's Medical Mysteries.

- http://www.attalus.org. A gateway to splendid chronologies and translations.

- http://www.3pipe.net. Explores women artists and women in art of earlier eras, especially medieval and Renaissance but also classical antiquity.

- http://www.vickileon.com. The author's own links and bibliographies on her blog and website.

INDEX

In this index, major entries are boldfaced; dates in parentheses are labeled "a" for "active," and "c" for "circa" or "around." Many dates are approximate and some still disputed, such as Hatshepsut and other Egyptian 18th-dynasty women. Entries also include country of origin and/or locales associated with a given woman. Names (Beatrice, for example) had even more spelling variations than they do today.

A

Aahotep (queen) of Egypt (a. 1600 B.C.), 8

Aelfwyn of England (a. A.D. 1000), 67–68

Aethelfled of England (a. A.D. 900), 67–68

Agrippina the Younger (empress) of Rome, 40

Akiko, empress of Japan, 82

Al-Adawiya, Rabi'a of Persia (a. A.D. 750), 62–63

Al-Mustakfi, Wallada of Spain (a. A.D. 1040), 73–75

Al-Tayyani, Muhya of Spain, 74

Allerton, Mary of Holland and Massachusetts (a. A.D. 1620), 162

Amat-Mamu of Mesopotamia (a. 1770 B.C.), 6–7

Ana de Osorio of Spain (a. A.D. 1638), 145

Anguissola, Sofonisba of Italy (a. A.D. 1570), 127–28

Ankhesenamun (queen) of Egypt (a. 1343 B.C., dates disputed), 15–16

Aquilia Severa, Julia of Rome (a. A.D. 220), 45–46

Arete of Cyrene, North Africa (a. 380 B.C.), 26–27

Asellina of Pompeii, Italy (a. A.D. 78), 34

Ashley, Katherine Champernowne of England (a. A.D. 1570), 139–41

Aud the Deep-Minded of British Isles and Iceland (a. A.D. 900), 65–67